D0630716

A Conceptual Approach to Basketball

Vic Pruden

Leisure Press
Champaign, Illinois

Library of Congress Cataloging-in-Publication Data

Pruden, Vic, 1935-
A conceptual approach to basketball.

1. Basketball--Coaching. I. Title.
GV885.3.P76 1987 796.32'3'077 87-2671
ISBN 0-88011-287-5

Developmental Editor: Steve Houseworth
Copy Editor: Janis Young
Assistant Editor: Janet Beals
Production Director: Ernie Noa
Assistant Production Director: Lezli Harris
Typesetter: Theresa Bear
Text Design: Keith Blomberg
Text Layout: Denise Peters
Cover Design: Conundrum Designs
Illustrations By: David Hewlett
Author Photo (p. 108): Courtesy *Brandon Sun*, Brandon, Manitoba
Printed By: Braun-Brumfield

ISBN: 0-88011-287-5

Printed in the United States of America

10 9 8 7 6 5 4 3 2 1

Leisure Press
A division of Human Kinetics Publishers, Inc.
Box 5076, Champaign, IL 61820
1-800-DIAL-HKP
1-800-334-3665 (in Illinois)

Dedication

To my wife, Doreen, who loved me through the best and the worst of 20 basketball seasons.

Acknowledgments

The thoughts in this book come from my 25 years of successful coaching experience. I am indebted to the coaches, players, and friends in other disciplines who have supported me when I needed support and have challenged me when I needed the challenge.

Contents

Foreword

When I was a youngster, basketball appealed to me because of its simplicity. I could run, jump, dribble, and shoot. I could play with teammates, one-on-one, or alone. I loved the challenge of the ever-changing pace from offense to defense. As a coach, I try to remember the fun of playing basketball and strive to keep it simple and fun for my players as well. My success as a coach is largely due to the fact that I make basketball simple and relevant to my players. Through trial and error (a lot of error), I realized that complex playing systems could only confuse the opposing team if I could simplify these systems enough to teach them to my own team. My years of experience made the playing systems seem perfectly simple and straightforward to me. I failed to realize that not every player has the experience and insight to learn and implement playing systems as fast as we coaches would prefer. Rather than teaching sophisticated playing systems, I really needed to teach my players the nature of basketball, knowledge I had accumulated over several decades. Eventually, I began to teach playing systems as part of basketball concepts and playing principles. Thus, as my players understood more fully the nature of basketball play, they were able to learn more complex playing systems, to play more spontaneously, and most of all to have more fun.

What separates great players from good and mediocre players is spontaneous, skillful, and effective play. Less talented players with understanding and insight, or *court sense*, often perform better than more talented players with no court sense. Its easy to identify players with court sense: They seem to know what to do, are able to anticipate plays, and all the time enjoy themselves. Think of your team's potential if all the players had *court sense*. Vic Pruden's *A Conceptual Approach to Basketball* can help your team develop court sense by showing you how to share your experience. A highly respected and successful basketball coach in Canada, Vic has formalized basketball concepts and principles and presented them in a style that is straightforward and easy to understand. Have you ever wondered why your players seemed unable to grasp the plays you rehearsed over and over again? If you know your team has more ability than it exhibits, I highly recommend this book. It will help you share your experience with your players and simplify the complexity. After all, basketball is a simple game! And simple games are fun to play and to coach.

Jack Donohue
Head Coach
Canadian Men's National Basketball Team

Preface

Basketball has something for everyone. People of all ages can play. The game provides a satisfying leisure activity as well as an excellent vehicle for physical fitness and an outlet for highly competitive people. Basketball, therefore, is a flexible game.

Basketball is also a multifaceted game. Because the rules of the game limit the amount of physical contact and how a player may advance with the ball, basketball is as much a game of skill and finesse as it is of athletic prowess and agressiveness. I am always amused that our university faculty team, made up of mostly middle-aged ex-players with spare tires and well-used muscles, usually wins games against teams of undergraduates with young bodies and boundless energy. Furthermore, although basketball is usually thought of as a team game, it can be played one-on-one. It can also be a game for one person—all a player needs is a ball, a basket, and some imagination. I still enjoy putting the ball into the hoop, particularly when I create an imaginary situation like sinking the last-second winning field goal or the winning free-throw.

Basketball is challenging. For me, first as a player and later as a coach, the essence of basketball has been to play well. The experience of knowing that you are playing well is one of satisfaction, joy, and exhilaration. The ultimate experience is playing well and winning, too.

Because playing well occurs when performance reflects a generally accepted concept of how basketball should be played, people who influence how basketball is played, who want to play basketball well, and who enjoy watching basketball that is well played should have such a concept. This book, therefore, is about "how basketball should be played." Its purpose, however, is not to provide a blueprint for playing basketball; it offers no patterned offenses, patterned defenses, or set plays. Rather, my intent in writing this book was to present the validity of designing systems of play that are predicated on universal ideas. I also wanted to share some of my ideas that may have universal application in the design of a coherent overall system, consisting of offenses, defenses, and the various skills of the game. Such ideas can also be used as a touchstone for judging not only the quality of the design of a particular system, but also the quality of player performance in a game.

This book was written primarily for coaches. I trust the ideas it explores will prove useful to those who are coaching basketball for the first time as well as to more experienced coaches who are constantly honing their ideas through a continuous process of self-appraisal. This book is also for players, parents, and others who wish to gain insight into how basketball should be played.

Chapter 1

The Need for a System of Play

A Coach's Dilemma

Basketball is a game for the mind as well as for the body. As a game for the mind, basketball requires players to make choices. During the course of play, they must select the most appropriate task to execute from a variety of possible tasks. This thought process resembles a multiple-choice quiz with a number of possible answers ranging from the least appropriate to the most appropriate. For example, each time players receive a pass within their shooting range, they have three basic options—to shoot, to pass, or to dribble. On the basis of a number of variables—such as their ability to shoot, to pass, and to dribble—they must select the most appropriate play option to execute. This selection process is not easy in a game of continuous play in which opponents are free to interfere with their play. Having made a choice, the players must physically execute it. Thus basketball is also a game for the body.

When I first began coaching, I made most of these choices for my players. They merely carried out my directions. I decided which players should shoot from the perimeter and from where on the perimeter they should shoot. I allowed only certain players to dribble the ball up the court and told others to play near the basket, to shoot only lay-ups, and to rebound. For some, this approach was comforting because they did not have to think; they simply followed orders. They could leave their creative minds in their lockers with their street clothes. However, those players who saw an opportunity to play creatively, perhaps by gaining an advantage over an opponent in some other way than I had designed, must have felt extremely frustrated.

I was never happy merely choreographing play for my players because that robbed them of the opportunity to exercise, test, and extend their full powers of will and intellect. As a result, despite our success at winning games, I became more and more vexed by the contradiction between the reasons *why* I chose to coach basketball and the *way* I coached it. On the one hand, I wanted to coach because basketball provided players with the opportunity to interact spontaneously, imaginatively, and creatively with opponents. On the other hand, having them play in my image continually limited or denied them the opportunity to play freely against their opponents. During the course of a game, I would analyze a situation and then tell them how to cope with it. For example, if an opposing team used a particular defense, I told my players how to attack it. By continually guiding the movement and actions of my players, I made them depend on me to tell them how to play. As a result, rather than freeing them to make their own decisions, I was reinforcing their dependence on me.

Resolving this dilemma became as important to me as winning games. The years that followed were truly challenging for me as well as for those young men and women who had to suffer the vicissitudes of my coaching as I searched to find a way of playing basketball that would make the game theirs in mind as well as in body.

Resolving the Dilemma

Although I wanted my players to play freely against their opponents, I also wanted them to play with discipline. If individual players were to fully exploit the opportunities that chance or their opponents provided for getting the ball or for scoring, each of them had to play with spontaneity, imagination, and creativeness. For team play to be effective, however, the players' movement and actions had to be integrated and coordinated into a coherent whole. If their movement and actions were to be in concert on every part of the basketball court, they had to play according to a mutually agreed upon and understood way of playing basketball.

For years, I searched for a way of playing that would fully reconcile these two apparently contradictory qualities of release and restraint. I finally discovered that a conceptual system of play not only offers the greatest potential for providing players with the freedom to make their own decisions on the court, but also helps them to play with discipline.

The Essential Nature of a Conceptual System of Play

A system of play predicated on a conceptual approach to play consists of ideas. Because ideas can be shared, everyone on a team has instant and equal access to them. As a result, these ideas—not the personal perceptions of a coach—guide the players' movement and actions. The rules of the game, which form part of this complex of ideas, have always served to guide the movement and actions of players. For example, the rule that deals with the restrictions placed on the footwork of a player with the ball determines how a player with the ball advances. After players have learned this rule, they do not need a coach to tell them what to do when they wish to advance the ball.

A conceptual system does not emphasize learning set plays choreographed by a coach or playing the game through the eyes of a coach. Instead, this system focuses on learning ideas about "how the game should be played" and on playing the game using one's own perceptions. Consequently, the players are free to make their own decisions as play unfolds, provided their movement and actions are consistent with clearly defined ideas and fall within the limits of their individual abilities. For example, because the ball can be advanced faster by passing than by dribbling, "look to pass before you dribble" is a general guideline in my system of play. If a player grabs a defensive rebound and has a clear path to the basket, he or she is free to dribble the length of the court and score—provided the player looks to pass before dribbling and is a proficient dribbler.

This way of playing in no way diminishes the responsibility of the coach to determine overall game strategy and to adjust that strategy during a game. Once the ball is in play, however, the players must make the decisions if they are to play with spontaneity, imagination, and creativity.

The Components of a Conceptual System of Play

A conceptual system of play consists of two categories of ideas: (a) ideas about the system's structure, which provide an overall framework for the movement and the actions of players and (b) ideas about how players should move and act within that structure.

The Structure of a Conceptual System

The structure of a conceptual system of play is an abstract model of all the possible movements and actions that players can execute during the course of play. This model consists of the playing area, offensive and defensive formations, and cues.

The basketball court serves as a grid for defining the precise location of players on the court. At any moment during play, players should know where they ought to be on the court.

Offensive and defensive formations are the means of organizing the movement and the actions of players within a particular formation on each part of the court as well as over the entire court. For each phase of play, these formations define the location of the players in relation to each other and to the court grid as well as the tasks that they must perform. For example, all players must know where to go and what to do after one of their teammates gets a defensive rebound. Each offensive and defensive formation is called a set.

An integral part of the structure is a mutually understood and agreed upon array of cues. Cues are signals that trigger the selection of the most appropriate movement or task to perform from a range of possible movements and tasks. For example, a pass that is initiated but not executed at the moment a player calls for the ball is a cue for the player who called for the pass to reverse cut.

Principles of Play

Ideas about how players should move and act within the structure are called principles of play. These principles are the means by which players can interact freely but with discipline with their opponents. As a result, players are free to (a) determine their own locations and movement patterns within particular offensive or defensive sets and (b) select the tasks to be performed, provided that all their movements and actions are consistent with these principles of play. In my system, for example, a player can shoot from the perimeter only if a teammate or teammates are in good position to get an offensive rebound should he or she miss the shot.

A Conceptual System and Player Development

I find, too, that using a conceptual system helps the development of young players. If coaches shared the same ideas about play, the experience that players have under one coach would help prepare them for the next grade or level of play. Because most players have different coaches at each grade or skill level, a conceptual system that helps players to understand the game and to adapt to various offenses and defenses will accelerate their development. For example, one of the first principles of play that all beginning players should learn is that immediately on gaining possession of the ball, they must look directly toward their basket for a teammate who may be open for a pass.

Flexibility of a Conceptual System

Conceptual systems of play predicated on a common set of ideas need not be alike; the design of each system will reflect the unique creative talent of the coach who designed it. Yet, although such systems will be as different from one another as the coaches who design them, they will all have a basic consistency that will benefit players. As a result, regardless of the age, the experience, the height, the athletic ability, or the skill of your players in a particular year, you should teach all of them ideas about play that have universal application. For example, the idea that a player should be able to dribble equally well with either hand is as relevant to a nine-year-old who is playing basketball for the first time as it is to a player in the National Basketball Association.

Chapter

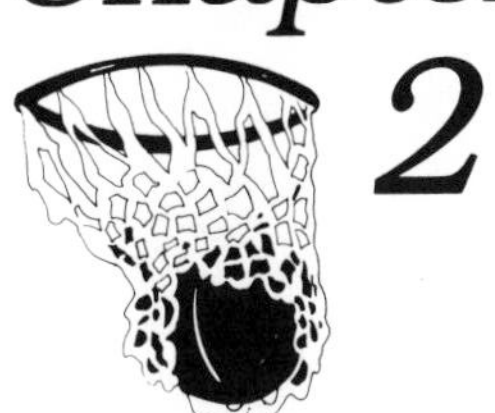

2

The Structure of a Conceptual System of Play

The Universal Elements of Structure

Information on particular offenses, defenses, and fundamental skills of the game is readily available in books written by successful coaches. In my view, however, the structures of all systems of play that successful coaches have designed share a number of common elements. These common elements serve as building blocks for the design of all systems of play. Knowledge of these building blocks provides a starting point for designing a coherent structure of play. These common elements are the court grid, offensive and defensive sets, and cues.

The Court Grid

The court grid is a vehicle that helps coaches to precisely define the location of players on the playing area. At any moment during the course of play, players should know where they should be on the playing area. The basketball court and both baskets constitute the basic grid (see Figure 2-1). In order to meet the unique needs of play on offense and on defense, this basic grid is further divided into an offensive and a defensive court grid.

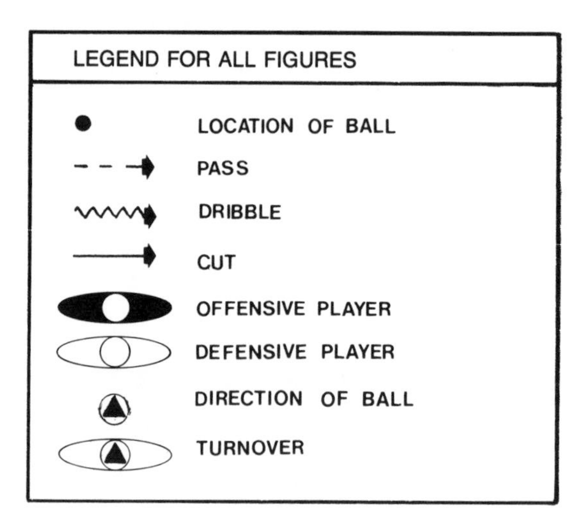

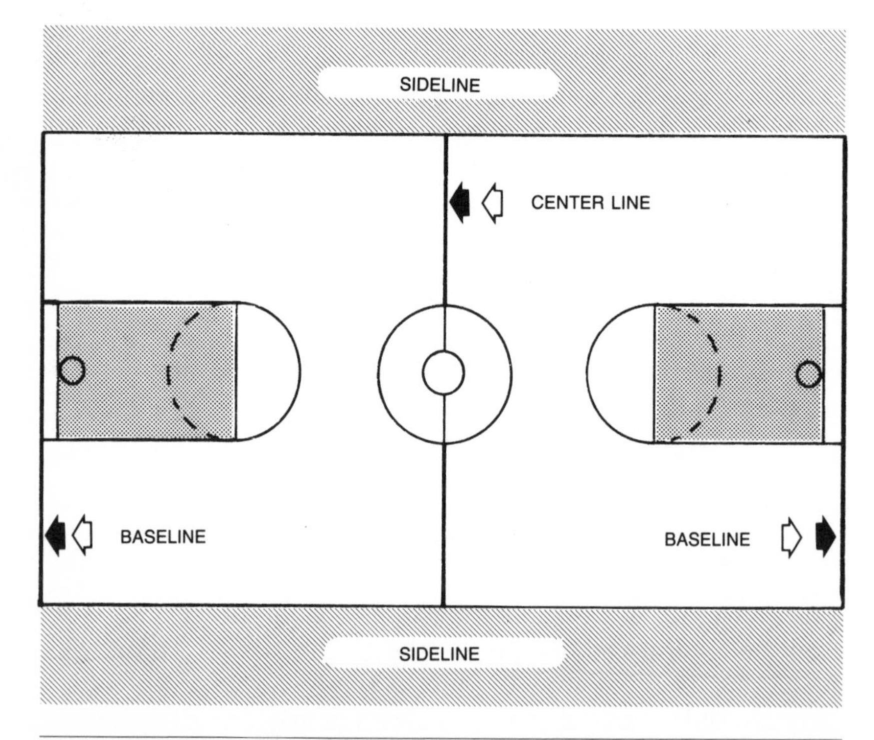

Figure 2-1 The Basketball Court.

The Offensive Court Grid

The offensive court grid divides the basketball court into four distinct playing areas: backcourt, frontcourt, midcourt, and full court. As shown in Figure 2-2, the backcourt is bounded by the baseline nearest the opponent's basket, by both sidelines, and by the center line.

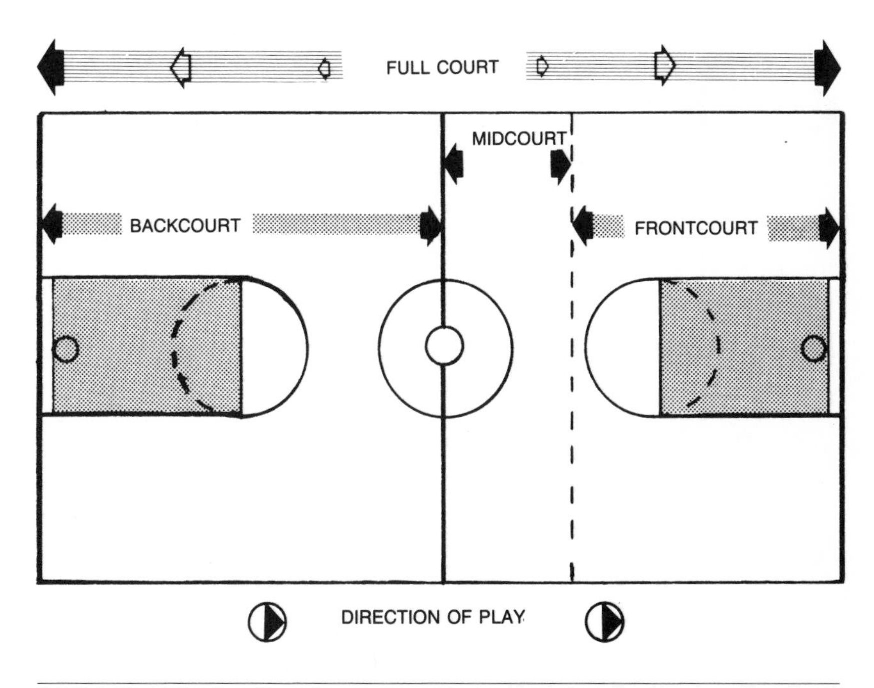

Figure 2-2 The Offensive Backcourt, Midcourt, and Frontcourt.

The frontcourt is bounded by the baseline nearest the basket at which a team is shooting, by both sidelines, and by a line running parallel to the baseline and roughly 28 feet from it.

The midcourt lies between the frontcourt and the backcourt. The backcourt, the midcourt, and the frontcourt make up the full court.

As shown in Figure 2-3, the full court is divided along its length in two ways. First, it is divided into a right half and a left half as a team faces its basket. Second, the full court is divided into three lanes of equal width—a middle lane and two side lanes.

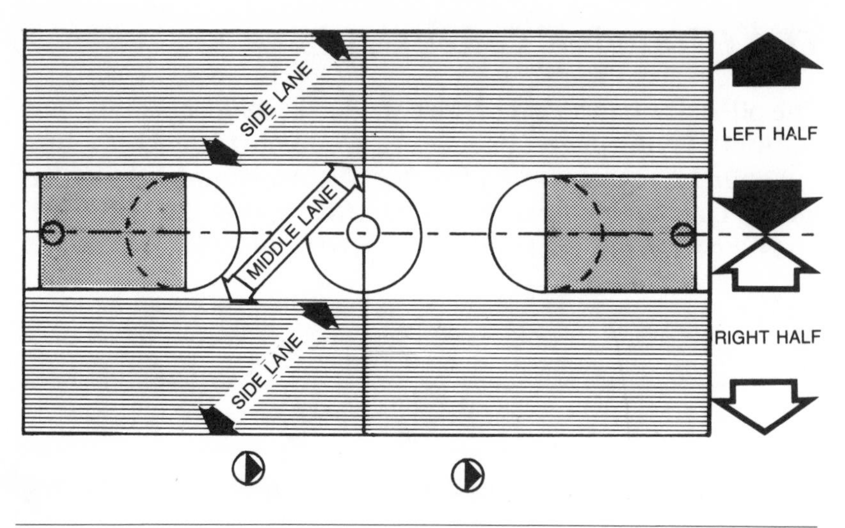

Figure 2-3 The Offensive Court Lanes.

The Defensive Court Grid

On defense, the basketball court is divided into five playing areas. Each playing area falls behind a line that marks the location on the court where the defense chooses to initiate team play against its opponent. Each line is called a front (see Figure 2-4).

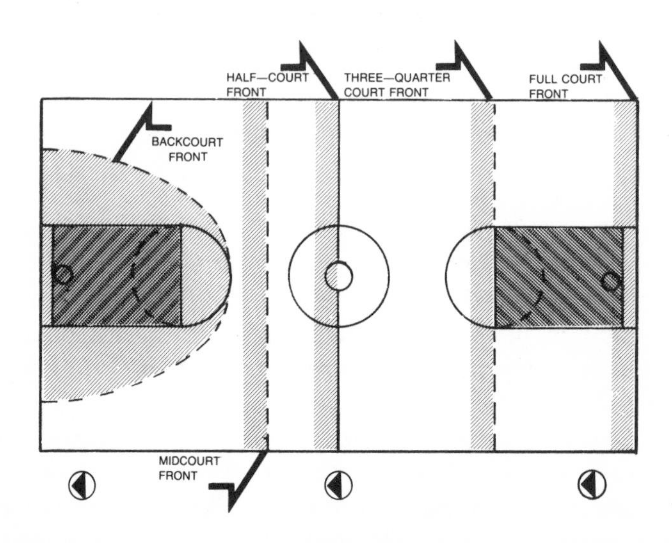

Figure 2-4 The Defensive Court Grid.

In a full court front, the defense challenges its opponents when they attempt a baseline throw-in after scoring or when they attempt to advance the ball immediately after gaining possession of a defensive rebound.

The three-quarter front is located along a line that corresponds to an extension of the free-throw line. The half-court front is located along the center line of the basketball court. Although the location of the midcourt front may vary, it always falls between the center line and the line 28 feet from the baseline in the defensive back court.

The backcourt front runs along an arc with a radius that extends from the opponent's basket to a point beyond which the defense will not challenge the offense. Depending on the strategy of the team on defense, this radius can be shortened or extended. The normal range for such movement is between 15 and 20 feet from the opponent's basket.

Offensive and Defensive Sets

If players are to integrate and coordinate their efforts on offense and on defense, they should know their location in relation to the court grid and also to each other. The set allows players to define this relationship. An offensive set is an arrangement of positions in relation to each other and to one of the playing areas of the offensive court grid. A defensive set is an arrangement of positions in relation to each other located behind a particular defensive front.

Positions

Although an abstraction, each position has a clearly defined role. As a result, as soon as a team either gains or loses possession of the ball, each member of that team must occupy a position in the appropriate offensive or defensive set. Each player, therefore, assumes the role that corresponds to the position he or she occupies. When players change positions, they change roles.

Consequently, if a player wants to play a particular position in an offensive or a defensive set, he or she must first learn the role assigned to that position and then work to execute that role proficiently.

Offensive and Defensive Roles

On offense, the role of all the players is directed to controlling the ball and to putting it into the basket at which they are shooting. Their role on defense is to prevent the offensive team from scoring. This is accomplished by interfering with their opponents' play by intercepting passes, and by keeping the ball and opposing players away from the basket. For example, if a player prefers to shoot from a particular location on the court, whoever is guarding that player must not let him or her shoot from that location.

Player Tasks

To fulfill their roles, players must perform a variety of tasks. These tasks include making decisions, executing a variety of one-on-one and team play options, and maintaining system integrity.

Decision-making requires players to perceive particular cues, to interpret them, and then to select the most appropriate movement or action to execute from a range of possible movements and actions.

One-on-one and team play options are tasks that require the execution of technically sound movement patterns or motor skills. One-on-one play options include all those tasks in which one opponent directly confronts and interacts with another. For example, driving is a one-on-one play action that involves dribbling the ball past an opponent.

Team play options require players to integrate and coordinate their movement and actions with those of their teammates, while also directly confronting and interacting with one or more opponents. For example, a double team occurs when two players on defense work together to guard one opponent. As the two players execute a double team, their teammates must provide support.

Proficient performance of one-on-one and team play options depends on the mastery of individual basketball skills. Players who have not developed a strong sense of spatial awareness may not be able to position themselves properly on the court or in a particular team formation. Players who have not developed a kinesthetic sense and motor control and who have not mastered such basic skills as dribbling, shooting, stopping, and pivoting are unlikely to proficiently execute one-on-one and team play options. For example, how can a player who must struggle to control the ball when dribbling focus attention adequately on the actions of the opponent guarding him or her, or on his or her teammates and their opponents? Because these individual skills are a prerequisite to proficient one-on-one and team play, they are called readiness skills.

Maintaining system integrity involves (a) being in the correct offensive or defensive phase of play, (b) selecting the appropriate offensive or defensive set, (c) knowing which position to occupy in that set, (d) knowing the role of that position, (e) knowing the role of each teammate, and (f) moving and acting in a manner that is consistent with the principles of play. In order to coordinate and integrate their efforts successfully while directly confronting and interacting with their opponent, players must be able to anticipate and prepare for what is going to happen next. This condition is possible only when players know each other's role. Proficient performance in team play, therefore, requires that players know what their teammates are likely to do in a particular situation. For example, knowing when to prepare to receive a pass is a function of knowing where and when to receive that pass and from whom. Furthermore, knowing the roles of all the positions gives a player the potential to play those positions; the more positions a player can play, the more valuable he or she is to the team.

Offensive Sets

The positions in an offensive set may be organized in a variety of formations. Each formation is described by using digits to represent the location of the positions in relation to each other.

For example, the numerical representation 2:1:2 describes the basic formation. Each set also has a suffix that tells us where the formation is located. For example, a 2:1:2 frontcourt set is a formation of positions in which there are two guards, one post, and two forwards. This 2:1:2 formation is located in the frontcourt.

Although sets are comprised of many different formations of positions, their location on the court grid determines their overall function. The functions of the various formations of backcourt sets, midcourt sets, frontcourt sets, and full court sets are described in the following sections.

Backcourt Sets

Play in the backcourt is directed to advancing the ball out of the backcourt within the 10 seconds allowed for this action. Because backcourt sets serve as a springboard for full court sets, they are often called outlet sets.

Midcourt Sets

As the ball enters the midcourt, the player with the ball must decide to execute a fast break triangle entry or a frontcourt entry or to keep the ball in the midcourt. A team may decide either to keep the ball in the midcourt or to return it to the midcourt from the frontcourt for a number of reasons. For example, should the team on defense change its defensive set, the opposing team may choose to move into another offensive set or to adjust the set it is using. Also, a team may decide to keep the ball away from the defense—that is, to stall or to freeze the ball. For example, if a team has a one or two point lead with a few minutes left on the clock, it may choose to keep the ball in the midcourt away from the opposing team until time runs out.

Frontcourt Sets

Frontcourt sets organize play near the basket at which a team is shooting in order to produce high percentage shots, offensive rebounding, and defensive balance. At the moment players anticipate that a teammate should be shooting, they provide the shooter with support. At least two players should work for a good offensive rebounding position. The other two should be ready to play defense in the event the opposing team gains possession of the ball. The player who is shooting should follow the shot to the basket for a rebound or provide defensive balance by occupying either the short or long safety position.

Full Court Sets

Full court sets organize play over the entire court grid—that is, from the backcourt through the midcourt and into the frontcourt. Their purpose is to help players exploit situations in which they outnumber their opponents. When players outnumber their opponents, they have an opportunity for an unguarded shot at or near the basket. Consequently, if players are to exploit these opportunities, they must be able to quickly perceive and react to occasions of numerical advantage. Because players must be quick to take full advantage of these opportunities, these sets are also called fast break sets. Play in the fast break set consists of three phases: the outlet phase, the penetration phase, and the fast break triangle phase.

The outlet phase. The outlet phase occurs in the backcourt. The opportunity to create situations in which players outnumber their opponents is directly proportional to the speed with which the ball is advanced from the backcourt. Outlet sets, therefore, must facilitate this phase of full court play.

The penetration phase. The penetration phase occurs as the ball enters the midcourt. At that time, the player with the ball must decide whether or not to penetrate by quickly advancing the ball with a pass or a dribble into the fast break triangle. Such penetration initiates play in the fast break triangle phase of the fast break set. On the other hand, should the player decide not to penetrate, he or she will either keep the ball in the midcourt or advance it into the frontcourt to initiate play in a frontcourt set.

The fast break triangle phase. The fast break triangle phase takes place in the frontcourt (see Figure 2-5). As the ball arrives at one of these positions from the midcourt with a pass or a dribble or directly from the backcourt with a pass, the player occupying that position must quickly shoot or make one pass that must be immediately followed by a shot. Should neither a shot nor a pass occur immediately after the ball first enters one of the three positions in the triangle, or should no shot occur immediately after the first pass from a position in the triangle, play in the triangle phase ends, and frontcourt play begins.

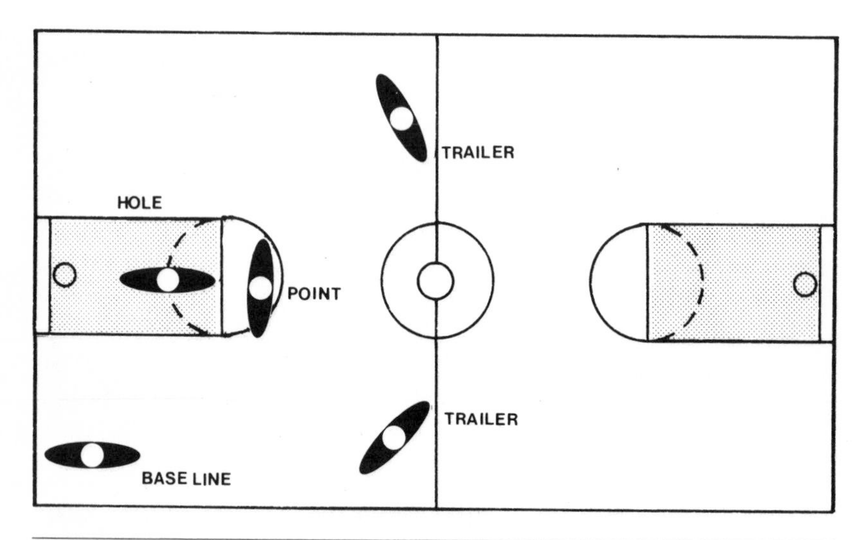

Figure 2-5 Offensive Positions for the Fast Break Triangle.

Defensive Sets

Defensive sets are defined first by whether they are zone sets, man-to-man sets, match-up sets, or combination sets and second according to the front behind which they are located. The terms zone, man-to-man, match-up, and combination denote a particular category of defense. Many variations exist within each category.

Zone Sets

In zone sets, players occupy positions in a specific formation. A player who occupies a position in a zone set is responsible for guarding a designated area behind a defensive front. The overall movement of the positions in the zone is in reaction to the location and the movement of the ball. As a result, each player is likely to face the ball. The players move in unison, adjusting their location each time the ball moves. Although the players focus intensely on the location of the ball, they are also responsible for opponents in their designated area. Within that area, the defensive player will attempt to keep the ball away from opponents or to stop players from cutting into the zone for a pass. The formations of zone sets are described by using digits. For example, the numerical phrase 1:2:2 describes the formation of the positions in a zone set.

Man-to-Man Sets

In a man-to-man set, players are responsible for guarding a particular opponent. As a result, the positions in a man-to-man set mirror the positions of the offensive set employed by the team on offense. Although the major role of each player is to guard an opponent, players must also know where the ball is and help their teammates.

Match-Up Sets

Match-up sets usually occur only behind a backcourt front. In a match-up set the players match up with the players on offense by playing man-to-man. However, as soon as the team on offense initiates play in their frontcourt set, the team on defense plays zone, using a formation that matches the one employed by the team on offense.

Combination Sets

A combination set is a composite of man-to-man, zone, and match-up sets. In a combination set, for example, a team may first match up and then play zone when an offensive player passes the ball to one side to initiate play in the frontcourt and switch to man-to-man when a player passes the ball to the other side to initiate play. Another example of a combination set occurs when some players play zone and others play man-to-man. Perhaps four players may play zone while the fifth plays man-to-man.

Cues

To integrate and to coordinate their efforts, players also need a mutually understood and agreed-upon array of cues that trigger selection of the most appropriate movement or task from a range of possible movements and tasks for each moment of play. For example, a pass that is initiated but not executed at the moment a player calls for the ball is a cue for that player to reverse cut. Before players can respond to these cues, they must know and understand them. Cues can be team-related, opponent-related, or event-related.

Team-Related Cues

Team-related cues include the actions and the characteristics of teammates, the actions of the coach, and the principles of play. The principles of play are examined in detail in chapter 3.

The actions of players include play options they may initiate or execute as well as a number of predetermined visual and auditory signals. A pass to a teammate is a play option that can cue a teammate to execute a basket cut, the classic "give and go." A visual cue is a player calling for the ball by raising his or her hand to indicate the spot or direction for the pass. When players use their voices to call for the ball, a screen, or a switch, they are using auditory cues.

Other team-related cues are the characteristics of teammates. Player characteristics include their physical, emotional, and intellectual strengths and limitations as well as the level of their proficiency in executing particular play options. For example, a player who executes a basket cut and who is open for a long pass may call for the ball. However, if that player has demonstrated through past performance that he or she is not likely to catch a long pass, the player with the ball should not pass it.

Opponent-Related Cues

The actions and characteristics of opposing players and the characteristics of their system of play provide cues. For example, players on your team may have noticed that a certain opposing player always brings the ball above his or her head before shooting and always lowers the ball below his or her waist before driving. Thus, the location of the ball is a cue that tells the defensive player what the player with the ball intends to do. Another cue is the situation in which a player on offense is guarded by a player who in some significant way is unable to match his or her abilities or characteristics. For example, the player on defense may be considerably shorter. This mismatch is a cue for the team on offense to exploit this situation by sending the taller player to the basket.

Event-Related Cues

Although event-related cues may be the result of an action by an opposing player or a teammate, they are separate from any such action. For example, ball possession and the location of the ball on the court grid are event-related cues. The act of getting the ball or losing the ball cues phase transition. Anticipating ball possession cues one team to begin to play offense and the other team to play defense. Further, the location of the ball on the court grid cues set selection. On offense, therefore, the ball entering the frontcourt cues the selection of a frontcourt set.

Chapter 3

The Principles of a Conceptual System of Play

Guiding the Movement and Actions of Players

You will recall that the purpose of a conceptual system of play is to allow players to play freely but with discipline. This discipline is provided by the structure and the principles of play of that system. Essentially, the structure provides an overall framework for the location, the movement, and the actions of players. This framework, however, is not rigid. Although players must move and act within it, they are free to choose, from a range of possible movements and actions, which particular movement or action to execute during each moment of play. As play unfolds, players are free to choose which offensive or defensive set to employ. To perform well, however, they must all be in the same offensive or defensive set. Within that set, players are free to choose which position to occupy and which movements and actions to execute while occupying a position.

These choices are guided by the principles of play as well as by the other team-, opponent-, and event-related cues. For example, one principle of play is that players should play within their limitations. As a result, a player who cannot accurately throw the ball the length of the court should not try to do so in a game.

These principles also serve as criteria not only for guiding *how* a particular movement or action should be executed, but also *when*. For example, if possible, a player should pass the ball to a teammate who is not closely guarded and who is within shooting range of the basket to ensure that the ball will be caught and shot in the shortest possible time. Passing in this way helps players to shoot before opponents can stop the shot or interfere with it. A player who is advancing the ball with a dribble and who is outside his or her shooting range should not simultaneously stop and end the dribble. He or she should keep dribbling. Ending the dribble outside shooting range allows the defensive player to drop off to help his or her teammates, because having ended a dribble, a player cannot dribble again and need not be so closely guarded.

The purpose of this chapter is to provide examples of the most salient principles of play of my conceptual system. These principles are divided into three categories: general principles that apply to both offense and defense, offensive principles, and defensive principles.

General Principles of Play

A number of general principles of play that guide decision making on both offense and defense are (a) flow, (b) tempo, (c) potentiality, (d) balance, (e) sequencing, (f) symmetry, and (g) initiating.

Flow

Team play and the execution of team and one-on-one play options should be smooth, continuous, and quick. This quality of play is called *flow*. Phase transition should occur at the moment players anticipate a change in ball possession. As a result, they should begin play on offense or on defense as soon as they anticipate either gaining or losing possession of the ball. The two tasks that initiate play in phase transition are selecting the appropriate offensive or defensive set and occupying a position in that set.

Set transition occurs each time a team moves from one phase of play to another as well as each time it changes either from one offensive set to another or from one defensive set to another. Each change can occur within a particular part of the court grid, such as the frontcourt, or when a team advances the ball from one part of the grid to another. For example, as players advance the ball into the frontcourt from the midcourt, they must move from a midcourt set into either the fast break triangle or a frontcourt set. Should the players move into a fast break triangle but fail to shoot immediately after the ball enters one of the positions in the triangle or after the first pass from that position, they must then move into a frontcourt set.

The articulation among the component parts of team and one-on-one play options ought to be smooth, continuous, and quick. For example, when dribbling, a player should end the dribble at the moment he or she selects a play option to initiate. Should that player choose to pass, the time interval between ending the dribble and passing should be as short as possible. His or her teammates should know which option the player is likely to initiate so that they can integrate their efforts with his or her effort.

Timing is important to flow. A player must execute play options at the appropriate moment in order for them to be effective. For example, a player should pass so that the ball arrives at the moment and the place the receiver expects it. As a result, players without the ball need to focus their full attention on the player with the ball only when they expect to receive a pass. At other times, they are free to focus their attention on what the defense and their teammates are doing. Knowing what the defense and teammates are doing provides players with cues that help them to select the appropriate play option and to integrate their movement with their teammates' movement.

Tempo

Tempo is the rate of speed at which players play basketball. Players should try to play at the highest possible speed. On the other hand, speed alone can be counterproductive. Just as the rate of speed at which a person drives a car should depend on road conditions and the driver's skill and experience, so the rate of speed at which teams play basketball should be determined by such variables as game strategy and the players' skill and experience. As a result, the tempo of play should be increased at certain times and decreased at others. A change in tempo may be dictated by the score and the time remaining in the game. With a minute or so remaining in the game, a team with a one or two point lead is likely to slow the tempo to allow time to run out.

At other times, the skill and experience of the opposing players will dictate the tempo. When the tempo of play increases beyond the skill and experience levels of a team, the quality of its play deteriorates. Players will hurry their shots, commit rule violations, and throw inaccurate passes. As a result, a basic game strategy on offense and defense is to play at a tempo that is beyond the capabilities of the opponent. Conversely, a team with less experience or skill should attempt to slow the tempo of play to a level that, at best, will allow them to play on equal terms with their opponents or that, at least, will reduce the number of their opponents' scoring attempts and keep the score respectable.

Improving tempo by developing individual skills. The quickness with which a play option is executed is determined by the player's innate ability and skill efficiency. The best way to improve quickness in play option execution is to improve skill efficiency. Skill efficiency is the relationship between the speed with which a play option is executed proficiently and (a) the number of discrete body movements needed to execute that play option and (b) the range of motion of each discrete movement. Therefore, to execute a task at maximum speed all superfluous movement must be eliminated. For example, analyze a perimeter shot of a player who is unguarded to determine the number of his or her discrete movements from the moment of receiving a pass until the moment the ball leaves his or her hand. Suppose a player receives a pass and then pivots so that he or she is square to the basket when shooting. Analyze whether this pivot is necessary. If, for example, that player had squared off to the basket before receiving the pass, one movement could have been eliminated.

Shortening the range of motion of each essential discrete movement will also increase the speed of play option execution. Range is the distance needed to complete a particular motion. Because time is a function of distance, any shortening of the range of motion will result in a shortening of the related time interval. For example, after getting an offensive rebound, many players lower the ball to below the waist. This action provides opponents with an opportunity to steal the ball or to obtain a held ball. Lowering the ball also increases the range of motion for shooting, which increases the time required to shoot. Keeping the ball above the head, however, protects the ball and shortens the range of motion for shooting so that a player can shoot quickly.

Improving tempo through anticipation. Anticipating the earliest moment at which to initiate a play option is another important aspect of skill efficiency. In the 100-meter sprint, for example, the ability to run fast is of little consequence if the sprinter is disqualified by false starts. On the other hand, I suspect many sprinters run their best times when they anticipate the start. This ability to anticipate is critical to playing with speed. For example, players can increase the speed with which they initiate a fast break by beginning fast break play at the moment a teammate is likely to get a defensive rebound rather than waiting until after a teammate gets the rebound. Thus focusing on relevant cues and anticipating events facilitate tempo.

Potentiality

Perhaps the greatest challenge facing a coach is reconciling the need players have for immediate success in their play with their need for future success. To reconcile this dilemma, a coach must help players to play within their present limitations, while also facilitating their growth and development. A coach, for example, may help the tallest player on the team succeed by limiting his or her role on offense to rebounding and shooting lay-ups and free throws and, on defense, to playing near the basket in a backcourt zone set. However, the coach must also prepare that player for high school and college play, in which he or she may not be the tallest player on the team. To accommodate these two apparently contradictory needs, a coach must design a system that allows players to play within their present limitations while nurturing their growth and development.

Often, however, coaches choose a different approach to developing a system of play. Some develop their system after they assess the talent and abilities of their players. Those who can rely on recruiting players with particular abilities may recruit players who fit into their system. Although both approaches can be very effective for winning games, each does little to facilitate the growth and development of young and inexperienced players. A system of play that hides individual and team weaknesses and that highlights only those skills already performed well makes it difficult for players to improve their skills and to acquire new ones.

Within the context of education, at least, a more appropriate approach is one that allows players to play within their present skill limitations, while encouraging them to acquire new skills. In games, players should play within their limitations. Between games, however, they should dedicate themselves to acquiring new skills as well as to honing those already acquired. Thus a player who cannot dribble well with his or her left hand should avoid dribbling with that hand in a game. However, that player should work assiduously between games, continuing to exercise the right hand and also concentrating on becoming a proficient dribbler with the left hand. In games, the player should begin to dribble with the left hand when appropriate for his or her skill level. Unfortunately, too often players attempt only those skills that they can do well, easily, or immediately. This is particularly true of gifted athletes who often enjoy early success in play, not because they are skilled but because they are competing against average athletes. It is also true of players who, at a young age, are significantly taller than their peers.

In basketball, being "free" to play does not mean that a player is free to do whatever he or she prefers. Being "free" should mean that a player has no preferences. For example, a player who is free in dribbling can dribble equally well with either hand. The more a player prefers to dribble with one hand only, the less free he or she is. A player is free, therefore, only to the degree to which he or she has mastered all of the skills of the game.

Balance

To be proficient, players must learn to balance the various component parts of one-on-one and team play. This quality of play is called skill balance. In one-on-one play, skill balance occurs when a player maintains the same ball/body relationship when initiating the basic play options of passing, shooting, and dribbling. In team play, this quality occurs when a balance exists between offensive and defensive play, inside and outside play, and onside and offside play. To tie one-on-one and team skill balance together, each player must possess emotional balance.

One-on-one skill balance. In one-on-one play, skill balance occurs when the ball/body relationship is the same for initiating each of the basic play options of passing, shooting, and dribbling. This position is called the "home" or "set" position. Therefore going through the set or the home position is a prerequisite for initiating either a pass, a shot, or a dribble. Should the starting position for each basic play option be different, the defense, by perceiving these differences, will be able to anticipate what the player with the ball intends to do and adjust its play accordingly. If, for example, a player with the ball begins the jump shot by holding the ball above his or her head but begins a drive by holding it below his or her waist, the defensive player guarding him or her can move closer as that player raises the ball above the head and farther away as he or she lowers the ball to below the waist. The teammates of the defensive player can also make defensive adjustments. Any such advance notice of a player's intention is called telegraphing.

Team skill balance. In team play, skill balance involves balance between play on offense and defense, inside and outside play, and onside and offside play. When a team is on offense, it must maintain defensive balance by being ready to play defense as soon as it anticipates losing the ball. Conversely, a team on defense maintains offensive balance by being ready to play offense as soon as it anticipates getting the ball.

Inside and outside balance in frontcourt play is essential. To rely on scoring only from close to the basket allows the players on defense who are guarding perimeter players to cheat to the inside. When the defense cheats in this way, it is giving the team on offense perimeter shots. However, can the team on offense score from the perimeter? Similarly, if a team relies on outside scoring, the defense can challenge the offense's outside game. When that happens, can the team on offense go inside?

In the same way, if frontcourt players have a bias to only one side of the floor, the team on defense will bring help from the side away from the ball (the offside). When this occurs, the offense must be able to react by moving the ball from one side of the frontcourt to the other side before the cheating players can recover. This maneuver is called reversing the ball.

Maintaining balance between one-on-one play and team play is also important. Players, therefore, must integrate one-on-one play with team play so that when a player wants to pass to a teammate (a team play option), he or she is also ready to drive (a one-on-one play option), and when a player is driving, he or she is also ready to pass. For example, if the player with the ball telegraphs a drive, an opponent who is guarding a teammate of the driving player can drop off to help stop the drive. This action is especially successful if the opponent knows that the driving player does not look to pass when driving and that his or her teammates do little to get in good position to receive a pass from that player. Of course, why should the players on offense without the ball work to get into good position if they know that their teammate is not likely to pass once he or she puts the ball to the floor?

Emotional balance. An integral component of skill balance is emotional balance. Emotional balance occurs when there is harmony between the level of emotional arousal of a player and the demands of play. The rheostat for controlling emotional levels is the will. Players, of course, must know the appropriate level of arousal for each moment of play. Although emotional intensity will vary within each phase of play, play on defense generally calls for greater emotional intensity than does play on offense. For example, the player going for a loose ball or a rebound needs to be highly aroused, while the player who is advancing the ball with a dribble must have ice water in his or her veins.

Sequencing

All aspects of a system of play must be consistent with the rules of the game. The majority of these rules are straightforward and can be understood by reading the rule book. However, coaches and their players must have an especially clear and precise understanding of the rules that govern body contact and restrict the footwork of a player with the ball, because these rules are of singular importance to how basketball is played.

Sequencing is the process of making play option selection orderly. Therefore during each moment of play, every player should know the play options of the position he or she is occupying and their ordinal number for selection. As a result, a player who gets a defensive rebound knows to look to pass before dribbling. When that player looks to pass, he or she knows which position to look to first, second, and third.

If teammates are to integrate and coordinate their efforts, they must know the sequencing of play option selection for each position in a set. This information provides them with cues for decision making. As a result, because a teammate of the player getting the defensive rebound knows that the rebounder will look first to pass to him or her, he or she will work to be open for the outlet pass.

If players are to be innovative and spontaneous in their play, they should be free to initiate unsequenced play options. For example, a player who is unguarded in an offensive frontcourt set but who is not sequenced at the moment for a pass should be free to call for the ball. Although players are "free" to be innovative and spontaneous in their play, they are not "free" to be inept or irresponsible by calling for the ball all the time or trying to score by themselves each time they get the ball. To maintain integrated and coordinated play when a player executes an unsequenced play option, players must learn to switch assignments. Switching assignments is called stunting.

Symmetry

Symmetry occurs when the players on the court maintain the spatial relationships among the five positions as defined in each offensive and defensive set. At any particular moment during the course of play, therefore, the location of each teammate on the court grid is predictable. This knowledge frees players to focus their attention on the location of their opponents rather than on trying to find a teammate. For example, a passer can focus his or her attention on the opponent guarding the intended receiver rather than on the receiver. Many passes are intercepted when the passer who focuses his or her attention on the receiver does not see the defense. Because timing is an integral component of flow, maintaining set symmetry increases the probability of developing a high degree of flow in the execution of team play options. The distances among positions in a particular offensive or defensive formation are relatively constant, which facilitates the development of a high degree of timing in the execution of team play options.

Initiating

The player who initiates an action has an advantage over the opponent who reacts to that action. The reacting player, in a sense, is always having to overtake the initiating player. For example, imagine two players who are to sprint the length of the court. One of the players gives the signal to start, which, of course, gives him or her the advantage. Because of this advantage, a player should attempt to be an initiator when interacting with an opponent. Initiating a particular play option, however, does not commit a player to completing that option. For example, a player may initiate a pass but execute a shot. Faking, therefore, is initiating one play option but executing another.

Offensive Principles of Play

A number of principles of play are unique to play on offense. These principles include (a) pinning, which occurs when an offensive player makes at least one opponent guard him or her closely, (b) penetrating, which occurs when a player with the ball advances it directly to the basket, first with a pass and second with a dribble, (c) creating a passing lane, which occurs when a player without the ball creates an open lane between a teammate with the ball and him or herself, (d) passing away from the defense, which occurs when the player with the ball passes the ball to a teammate so that an opponent guarding the receiver will have the greatest difficulty in deflecting or intercepting the pass, and (e) relay passing, which occurs when a passer uses a teammate as a go-between to complete a pass to another teammate.

Pinning

Pinning occurs when an offensive player makes at least one opponent guard him or her closely. The purpose of this maneuver is to prevent situations in which one defensive player is able to guard two offensive players. Therefore when a player who is dribbling pins an opponent before passing to a teammate, the player guarding him or her cannot easily guard the pass receiver. However, should the dribbler pass before pinning, the opponent that should have been pinned is free to guard the pass receiver. For example, when attacking a zone set, the player responsible for advancing the ball (the point guard) must pin at least one opponent before passing to a teammate. In Figures 3-1(a) and 3-1(b), players in a 1:3:1 offensive set are attacking opponents in a 2:1:2 defensive zone set. As shown in Figure 3-1(a), the point guard, Number 1, passes to teammate Number 3 before pinning. The defensive player closest to the point guard can then move to guard player Number 3. Therefore if the point guard does not pin the top two players in the zone, the player in the middle and the two back players can concentrate on protecting the area around the basket, while the two top players can easily guard the three perimeter players.

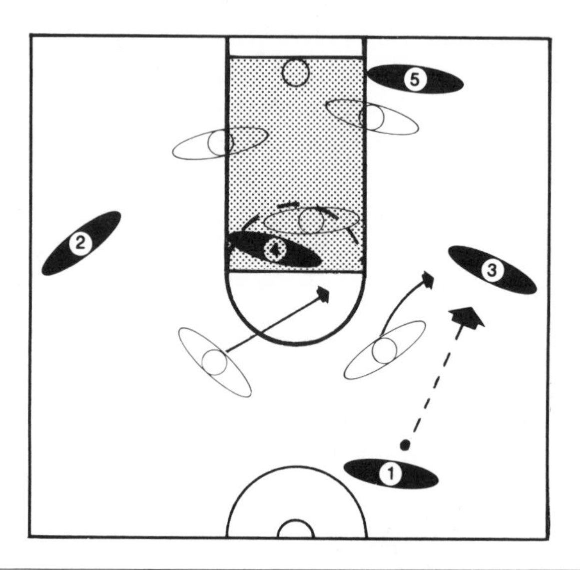

Figure 3-1(a) Attacking and Not Pinning the Defense.

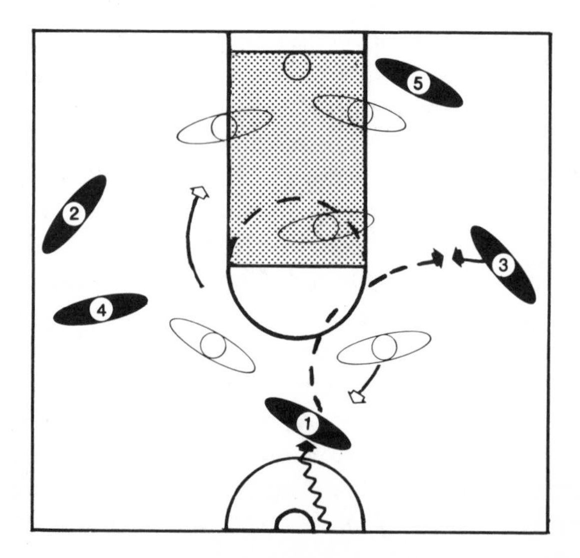

Figure 3-1(b) Attacking and Pinning the Defense.

However, as shown in Figure 3-1(b), when the point guard pins the top player before passing to Number 3, either the middle player in the zone or the onside back player of the zone set must guard player Number 3. This situation creates the potential to get the ball inside.

The player in position Number 3 should also pin by moving to within perimeter shooting range when the point guard is ready to pass. This forces the defensive player guarding player Number 5 into the difficult situation of having to guard two players at once, especially if player Number 4 pins the middle player in the zone. If the defensive player in anticipating a pass to the perimeter position moves toward that position before the pass, this two-on-one situation makes it possible for the point guard to initiate a pass to player Number 3 but deliver the ball to player Number 5 for an easy lay-up.

Penetrating

As soon as a player has possession of the ball, he or she should advance it directly to the basket, with a pass if possible and with a dribble if not. Advancing the ball directly to the basket is called penetrating. Because the middle lane provides the shortest and the most direct path to the basket, players should keep the ball in the middle lane of the court grid. Keeping the ball in the middle lane also provides access to both side lanes with relatively short passes (see Figure 3-2). On the other hand, when the ball is in one of the two side lanes, the offside lane is accessible only with a cross-court pass, which is a relatively long pass. As a result, when a player in a side lane chooses to execute a cross-court pass, he or she is asking for trouble, particularly when he or she passes the ball in front of a defensive player (see Figure 3-3). Only when a player cannot advance the ball in the middle lane should he or she use a side lane.

Creating Passing Lanes

To receive a pass, a player without the ball must create a passing lane between the passer and the spot on the court where

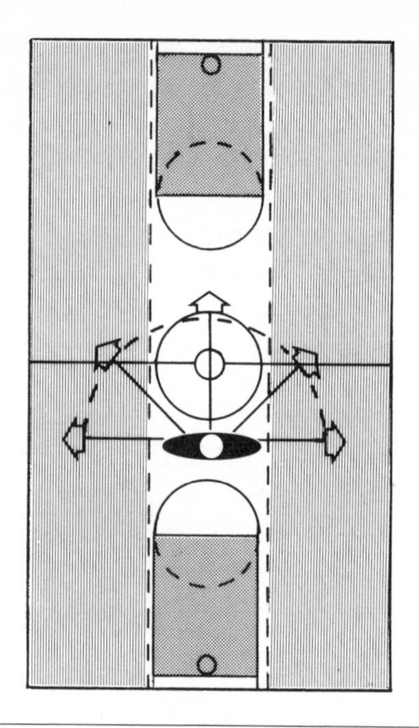

Figure 3-2 Keeping the Passing Lanes Short.

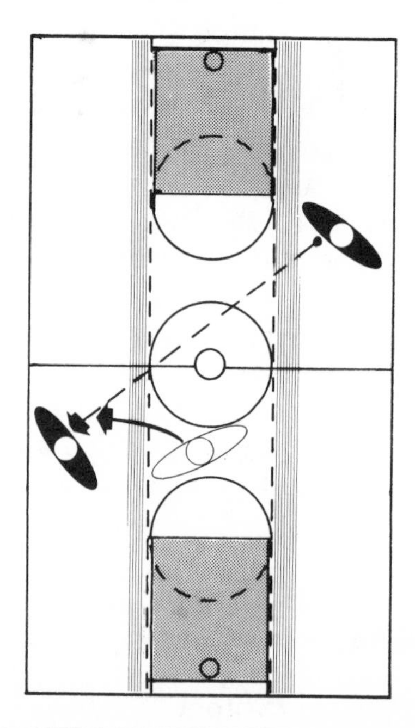

Figure 3-3 The Easily Intercepted Long Pass.

he or she wishes to catch the ball. When guarded closely by an opponent, a player without the ball must use his or her body to screen the opposing player from the spot on the court where he or she wishes to receive the pass. As a result, the defending player must go through the receiver to interfere with the pass. This maneuver is called sealing (see Figure 3-4). Also, instead of waiting for a pass, a receiver must move to meet it because waiting allows a defensive player to break the seal by moving around it.

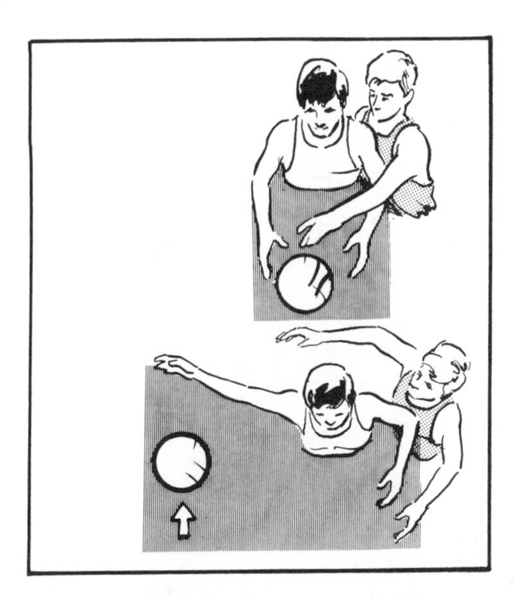

Figure 3-4 Sealing to Protect the Passing Lanes.

Passing Away From the Defense

When passing to a teammate, the passer must always pass the ball to the side that is away from the opponent rather than the side that is toward an opponent (see Figures 3-5 and 3-6). Passing the ball directly to a teammate makes it easier for a defender to reach in and knock the ball away. Passers should never pass the ball to a teammate at shoulder height where the defender can most easily interfere with a pass. As shown in Figures 3-7 and 3-8, the ball should always be passed high or low.

Figure 3-5 Passing Away From the Defense.

Figure 3-6 Passing to a Post Away From the Defense.

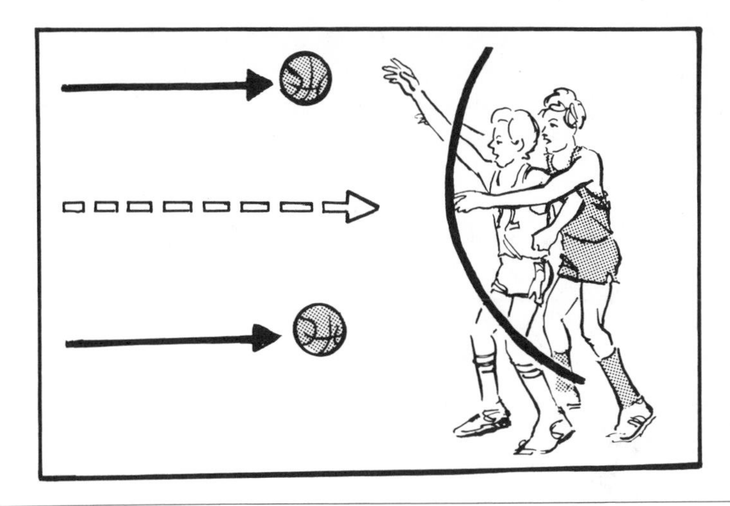

Figure 3-7 Making High Penetrating Passes.

Figure 3-8 Making Low Penetrating Passes.

Relaying

Relay passing occurs when a player cannot pass the ball directly to a teammate because an opponent is blocking the passing lane. When this situation occurs, the passer simply passes the ball to a teammate who relays it to the intended receiver before the defending player can block the new passing lane (see Figure 3-9). As a result, whenever a player cannot execute a penetrating pass, he or she should look to a teammate to relay the ball to the intended receiver. Often a relay pass is effective in the frontcourt when a player in the sidelane, trying to pass to the post, relays the ball to the point in reaction to a defensive player fronting the post (see Figure 3-9A).

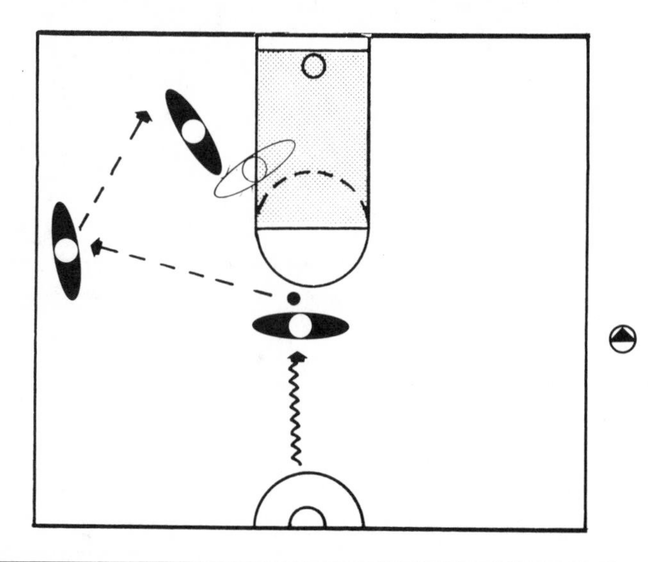

Figure 3-9 Relay Passing.

Figure 3-9(a) Defeating the Front.

Defensive Principles of Play

Three defensive principles of play are influencing, dropping to the ball, and helping and recovering. Players on defense must continually try to influence the movement and the actions of their opponents. Dropping to the ball is a principle that directs defensive players to select a location on the court in relation to the offensive player they are guarding, the defensive basket, and the ball. Players on defense must help each other. Such help, however, is conditional on their being able to maintain full defensive coverage. For example, as shown in Figure 3-10, a player who is helping to block a penetrating passing lane must be able to recover to stop the opponent he or she is guarding from shooting after receiving a pass.

Influencing

A corollary of the initiating principle is that each player on defense should not only look for every opportunity to stop opponents from scoring and to intercept passes, but also strive to influence both the opponent whom he or she is guarding and the other opponents away from their preferences.

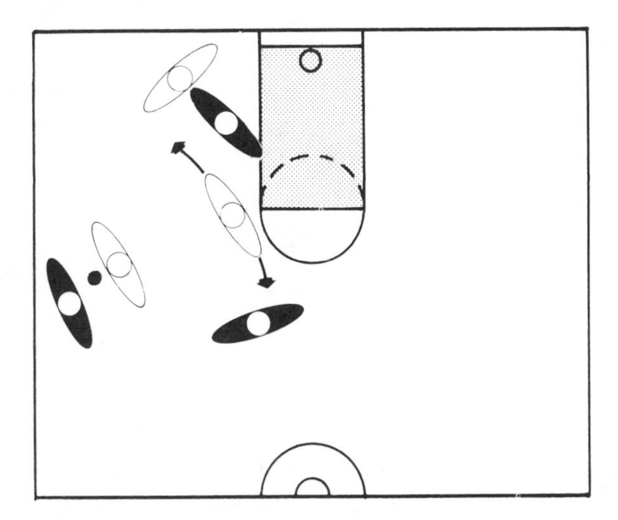

Figure 3-10 Helping to Block Passing Lanes.

Guarding a player with the ball. When guarding players who prefer to dribble with their left hand, defensive players should make them dribble with their right hand. If a player prefers to shoot a stationary jump, tell your players to make him or her shoot off a dribble. If a player prefers to shoot from a particular spot on the court, your players should make him or her shoot from another spot.

Guarding a player without the ball. A player guarding an opponent without the ball should occupy a position on the court that denies cuts to the ball and blocks passing lanes to the player whom he or she is guarding. Whenever possible, players should block cutting and passing lanes of as many opponents as possible.

Dropping to the Ball

Players who are guarding opponents without the ball must "drop to the ball." Players who are between the ball and the defensive basket must continually adjust their location on the court grid in relation to the distance between the players that they are guarding and the opponent with the ball. Therefore the greater the distance between a player with the ball and a teammate, the greater the distance should be between the defensive player and the player he or she is guarding.The drop to increase this distance is always toward the middle lane and the ball (see Figure 3-11). If the teammate of the player with the ball is behind the ball, the drop is always to get ahead of the ball and to double-team (see Figure 3-12).

The degree of drop is influenced by a number of variables, including the relative athletic ability and skill of the players and the style of play of the team on offense. For example, defensive players should watch for situations in which the player with the ball is guarded by a taller player. Because the player with the ball will experience considerable difficulty throwing long passes over the taller defender, teammates of that defender can execute a considerable drop to the ball, particularly when the player with the ball ends his or her dribble.

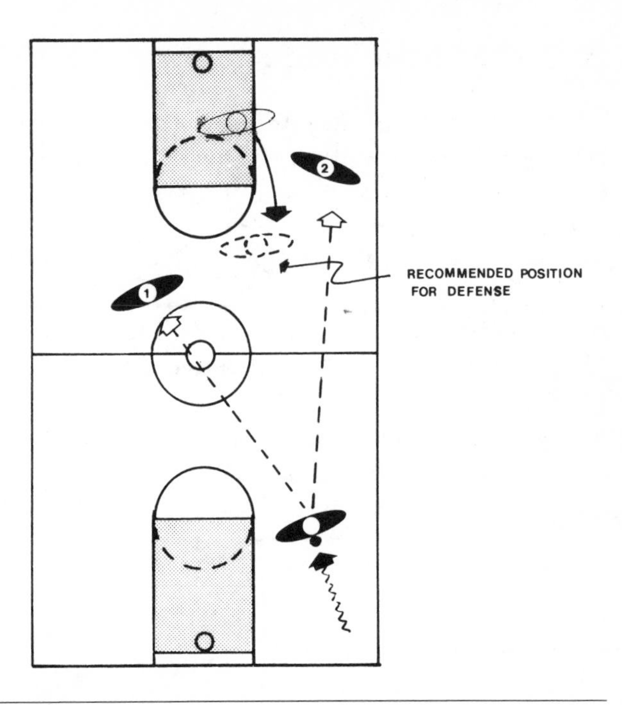

Figure 3-11 Dropping to the Ball When in Front of It.

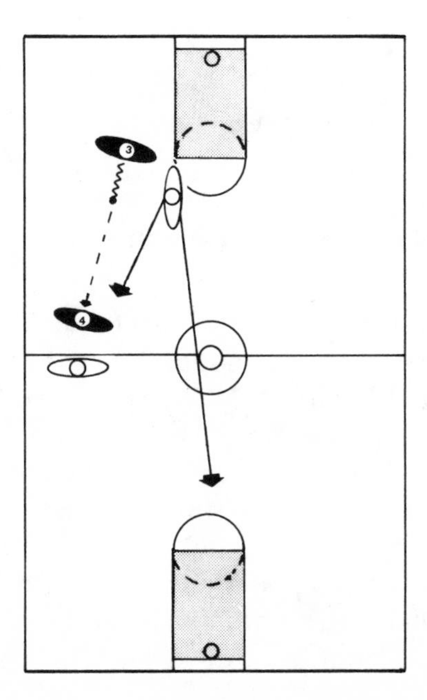

Figure 3-12 Dropping to the Ball When Behind It.

Helping and Recovering

While guarding an opponent without the ball, players must take every opportunity to help their teammates. Suppose, for example, that an opponent with the ball is initiating a drive. A teammate of the player guarding the driver may help by acting as if he or she is coming to guard the driver. As a result of this helping action, the opponent may decide not to execute the drive or, if he or she executes it, to end it early. Such help is particularly critical in a two-on-one situation. The single player on defense must limit the degree of penetration by the opponent who is open (see Figure 3-13) or try to slow the tempo of play until a teammate recovers to establish defensive parity.

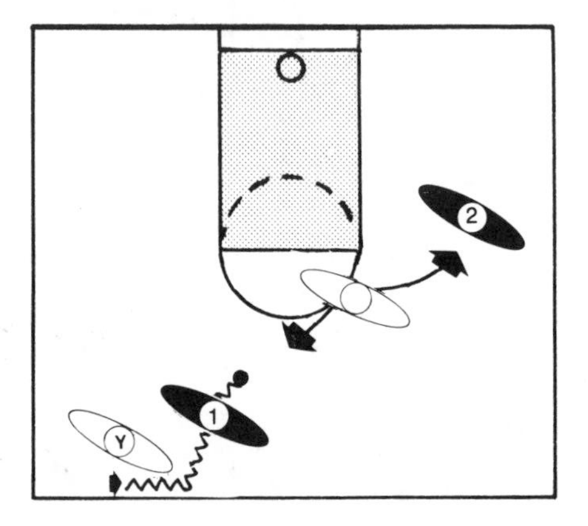

Figure 3-13 Helping to Slow Tempo and Limit Penetration.

The player guarding a player with the ball can also help his or her teammates. He or she should make every effort to block the high passing lane directly to the basket. This effort frees his or her teammates to overplay and front their opponents without fear of being burned by a reverse cut and a high pass to the basket for an easy lay-up.

However, players who are helping are still responsible for guarding their assigned opponent. Therefore the help a player gives to his or her teammates is limited to his or her ability to recover and to the amount of help teammates give that player.

Chapter 4

A Conceptual Approach to Offensive Team Play

Playing Against the Defense

More times than I care to remember, I have heard coaches and players attribute losing or poor performance to players not running their offense. Running an offense implies a "paint by number" approach in which players move according to a predetermined pattern. Their actions are programmed by set plays or the directions of the coach. Such an approach leaves little room for player spontaneity, creativity, and imagination. Players spend so much of their time learning how to run the offense that they tend to become "move players." A move player does things according to habit or involuntary reflex rather than choice. For example, as soon as some move players receive a pass, they fake one way and drive the other, no matter what their teammates or the opposing players are doing.

I refer to such players as "having paper bags over their heads." On one occasion, when my university women's team was practicing play in the frontcourt, I wanted to make one of the players who was playing a forward position aware that she was playing "with a paper bag over her head." She was not choosing a play option to execute by reading what the player guarding her, her teammates, and their opponents were doing. To make her aware of this, I asked the player who was guarding her to sit down cross-legged on the court at the moment the girl next received a pass from the guard. Sure enough, the next time she received a pass, the player who was guarding her sat down. The player with the ball faked a drive and faked a pass, only to be brought out of herself by the laughter of her teammates.

The principle of playing against the defense had occurred to me a few years earlier, when I was coaching university men's basketball. We were working on our frontcourt offense at practice. Play in the frontcourt was triggered by an entry pass from the guard to the forward. The guard brought the ball into the frontcourt and passed it to the forward. The player guarding the forward intercepted the pass. We started over. The defensive player intercepted the pass again. At this point, I began coaching and shouted at the guard, "What are you doing?"

The guard made the pass entry again. The defensive player intercepted the pass again. The guard pleaded, "How do you expect me to complete the pass when he knows that I'm going to pass?" My normal reaction would have been to instruct the defensive player to allow the entry pass so that we could work on our frontcourt offense. However, this time, in an inspirational moment, I asked the guard, "Whom do you watch when you pass the ball?" He replied, "The forward." I could not believe what I heard. Until that moment, I had assumed it to be self-evident that a player would read the defense before passing. I asked the other players on the team whether they watched the receiver or the opponent guarding the receiver when they passed the ball. Most of them replied, "The receiver."

Freeing Players to Play Against the Defense

If I wanted my players to read the defense before they executed a play option, I had to provide them with a way of playing basketball that would help them achieve that end. I concluded that it was unreasonable to expect a player with the ball to focus attention on both his or her teammates and the opposing players. The same is true for a player without the ball. He or she cannot give full and equal attention to the player with the ball and to the opposing players. The answer, I believed, lay in finding a way for players to focus more on the movement and actions of the opposing players than on those of their own teammates. I knew this was possible because I had experienced such a situation in high school when I played guard with a pal who played post. I would tell him where I wanted him to be when I drove to the basket. Because I knew where he would be, I did not need to watch him. I could focus my full attention on the opposing players. When my driving to the basket attracted his check, I passed the ball to him. Between us, we scored a great many points and won many more games than we lost.

Freeing Players With and Without the Ball

If the player with the ball and his or her teammates are going to be free to focus attention on the opposing players rather than on themselves, each of them must know exactly what the others are doing in terms of their location on the court grid and their movement. Simply put, if the player with the ball knows where his or her teammates are on the court grid and how they will react to defensive play, he or she does not need to concentrate fully on them. If the players without the ball know at which location on the court grid and when they are likely to receive a pass, each of them will know that he or she will not receive a pass unless he or she is in the right place at the right time to receive it. During this window of time, a player without the ball is free to read the cues provided by both teammates and opponents. For example, in my conceptual system of play, a player who is occupying a perimeter position in a frontcourt set and who is sequenced to receive a pass knows that he or she will receive a pass either in the perimeter position or in the "hole" and not in between (see Figure 4-1). As a result, while working to get open for a pass, the player does not need to concentrate fully on the player

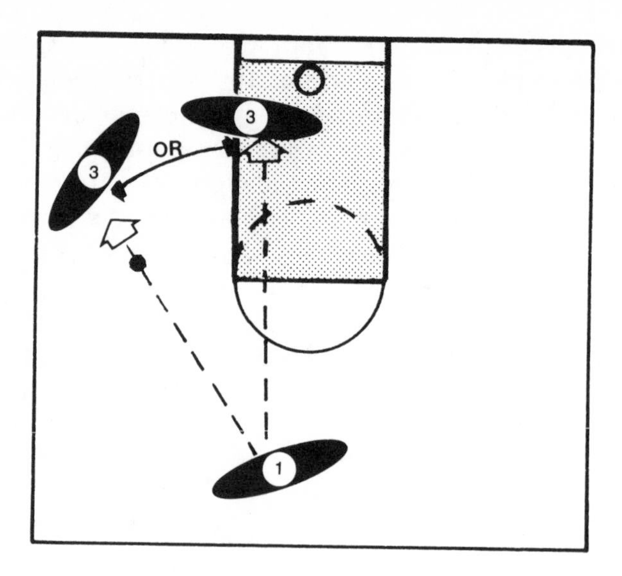

Figure 4-1 Knowing Where to Pass.

with the ball but on what the player guarding him or her is doing as well as on what players away from the ball are doing.

Playing against the defense implies that players are continually trying to exploit opportunities provided by chance and their opponents for advancing the ball and for scoring. As a result, players who play this way require no set pattern and no set plays.

Being a Gopher

Little burrowing animals called gophers live on the prairies, sitting for hours on their haunches contemplating the world. I refer to players as gophers if they separate reading the defense from initiating play options. Gophers will end their dribbles suddenly and then try to figure out what to do. After receiving a pass, gophers will lock their knees and hold the ball above their heads and wait. I sometimes think that they are waiting for divine intervention. Others will receive a pass, bend at the waist, and then swing the ball back and forth.

Perhaps they believe that this maneuver will mesmerize the defense.

Unfortunately, basketball is not like baseball, golf, or bowling. A clock is running. As a player, I wanted to play. As a result, I resented teammates who wasted time because they robbed me of playing time. As a spectator, I want to see action—not gophers. Gophers make the game ugly.

Because players should play with speed and initiative, they should initiate a play option at the moment they receive a pass, reading the defense as they initiate. This reading determines whether or not they should execute the option they initiate or switch to a suitable alternative. For example, a player in a side lane whose first play option is to execute a relay pass to a teammate in the middle lane should initiate that pass at the moment he or she receives the ball. However, execution of the pass depends on reading both the teammate who is receiving the pass and the defense.

A move player or a gopher will often initiate a pass only when he or she intends to pass. Because this behavior is a cue for the player guarding him or her to block the passing lane, the defensive player can interfere with the execution of the pass relatively easily. However, if the passer initiates that pass every time he or she gets the ball without necessarily executing a pass, the defensive player guarding him or her and the other defensive players cannot accurately predict what the player with the ball will do. As a result, should the defense try to interfere with the pass, the player with the ball can simply execute another play option. If the defense does not block passing lanes, the player with the ball will execute the pass.

Also, a player who is dribbling should initiate a play option only immediately after ending a dribble. The player, therefore, should not stop dribbling until the moment he or she chooses to initiate a shot or a pass. Thus the time interval between ending the dribble and either shooting or passing will be as short as possible. The shorter the time interval, the better the flow and the quicker the tempo of play. These two qualities of play make it harder for the defense to interfere with play; the less time opponents have to make defensive adjustments, the less opportunity they have for interfering with offensive play.

Knowing the Offensive System of Play

If offensive players are to play freely but with discipline against their opponents, they must know the offensive structure of a conceptual system of play and the principles of play that guide their movements and actions within that structure. They must also know how to use this knowledge. Without knowing the structure and the principles and how to apply them, players will not be able to integrate and coordinate their efforts effectively.

To test whether or not my players knew what to do during each moment of play, I would regularly blow a whistle to freeze their movement and actions at practice when we were working on team play. Then I would ask particular players to describe to me what they had done just before the whistle blew and whether or not their movement or action was consistent with our structure and principles of play. I would also ask players to tell me what a teammate or an opponent was doing and whether that player was doing what he or she should have been doing. This practice is very effective in helping players to use their minds as well as their bodies.

Knowledge related to structure includes (a) knowing how to select an offensive set, (b) knowing how to select a position, (c) knowing the tasks assigned to each position, and (d) knowing the cues and where to look for them.

Knowing How to Select an Offensive Set

If your team is to execute phase transition from defense to offense with speed, your players must know which offensive set to select at the moment transition occurs. Two factors influence this selection process—the location of the ball on the court grid at the moment of ball possession and the defense used by the opposing team. My system of play, for example, has a basic offensive set for each of the four areas of the offensive court grid: (a) the outlet set, (b) the midcourt set, (c) the frontcourt set, and (d) the full court set. As a result, when phase transition occurs in the backcourt, my players select the corresponding set, which is the outlet set.

Regardless of the defenses that teams employ during the course of a game, we use the same basic offensive sets against them. Although the basic formation of positions remains the same in each basic set, players learn to vary position location, position selection, play option sequencing, and play option selection. This flexibility allows the players to adapt their play within each basic set to any defense. As a result, rather than using a specific offensive formation for each defensive formation and then running fixed patterns or set plays, my players use the same basic formation but vary their movement and actions within it after reading the defense. Because we do not have particular offenses to match particular defenses, my players can begin to play against the defense at the moment they obtain possession of the ball.

Because phase transition can occur in a variety of ways, each basic set will require some modification to accommodate the different ways play begins in that set. Each of these ways is called an entry. For example, as shown in Figures 4-2, 4-3, and 4-4, the outlet set is modified to accommodate several

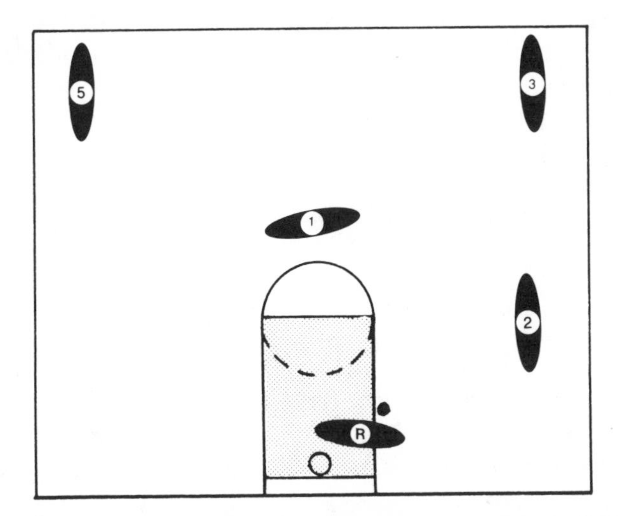

Figure 4-2 Defensive Rebound Entry (R) to the Outlet Set.

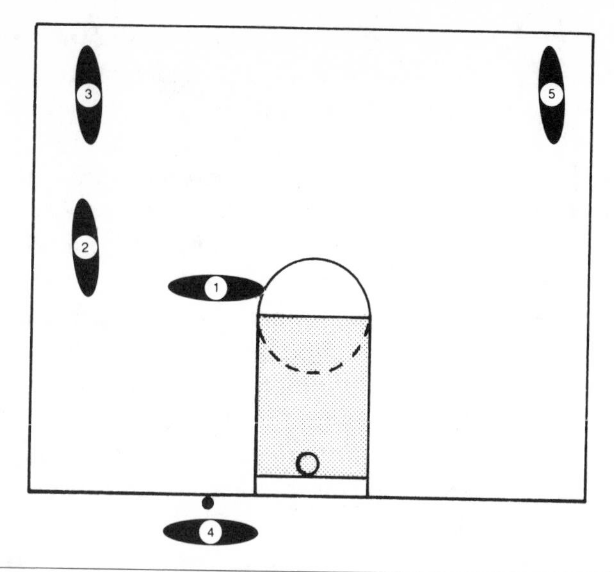

Figure 4-3 Baseline Throw-In Entry to the Outlet Set.

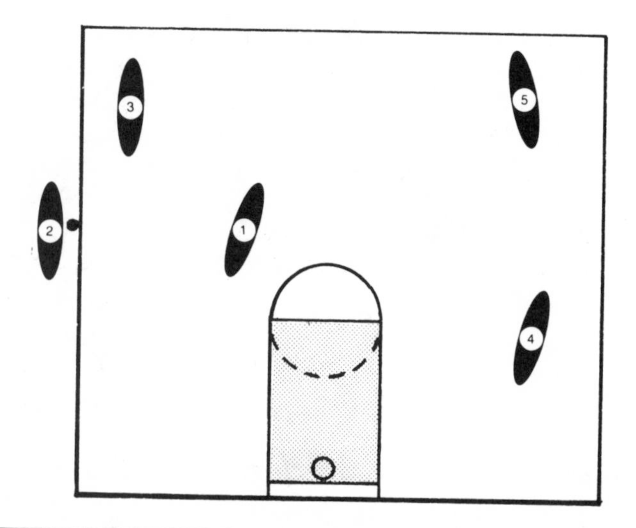

Figure 4-4 Sideline Throw-In Entry to the Outlet Set.

such entries: a defensive rebound, a baseline throw-in, and a sideline throw-in. The basic outlet set is shown in Figure 4-5.

Because the location of the ball on the court grid determines the offensive set my players use, the ball entering one area of the court grid from another area is a cue for my players to

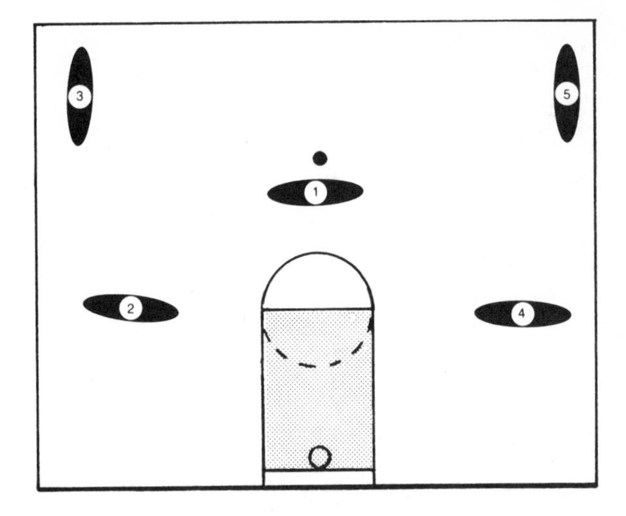

Figure 4-5 The Basic Outlet Set.

change from one set to the other. For example, a pass entry from the backcourt to the frontcourt cues the selection of the basic frontcourt set.

Knowing How to Select a Position

Concurrent with selecting an offensive set, players must select a position within that set. There are several ways to cue position selection. One way is to assign positions so that when players anticipate ball possession, they simply occupy their assigned positions. Another way is to allow players to occupy positions on a first-come, first-served basis. As a result, a position belongs to whichever player occupies it first.

Neither approach is satisfactory. The first approach is too limiting. It lessens the potential of the team and compromises player development. A team in which players are assigned to particular positions is characterized by play that is neither flexible nor spontaneous. For example, on many teams only one player is allowed to advance the ball from the backcourt. Because teammates always look to give the ball to him or her, they may forfeit many fast break opportunities with other players. Also, a team that relies on only one player to advance the ball is more vulnerable to defensive strategies than is a team that employs team play to advance the ball.

Players who play only one position become severely handicapped. I can remember a player in college who became upset when I asked him to play guard on the right side of the court during tryouts. Apparently, in high school, he had always played guard on the left side.

Because I have never been blessed with a team in which all the players could play every position equally well, allowing players to select positions on a first-come, first-served basis would have been a noble but foolish gesture. As a result, I developed another way of selecting positions that incorporates both assigning players to positions and allowing them to select positions on a first-come, first-served basis.

I call my approach grouping. In grouping, the five offensive positions are divided into groups of three and two, four and one, or two, two, and one. Players are then assigned to a particular group. Sometimes a group has only one position. When a group has two positions, I may either assign each player to a particular position or allow them to occupy the two positions on a first-come, first-served basis. When a group has three or more positions, I may assign players to positions, allow them to occupy the positions in their group on a first-come, first-served basis, or combine these two approaches. For example, if a group has three positions, one player may be assigned to one position and the other two players may be free to occupy the remaining two on a first-come, first-served basis. When players acquire the skill and the experience to play in every group of positions of an offensive set, they can—under clearly defined conditions—switch groups or stunt.

In my system of play, the five positions in each basic set are divided into two groups. One group consists of three positions and the other of two. For example, in the outlet and the midcourt sets, the group of three positions is the strong side and the group of two positions is the weak side. The players occupying the strong-side positions are responsible for advancing the ball, while the weak-side players provide support (see Figures 4-6 and 4-7).

In the basic frontcourt set, the strong-side players occupy the three perimeter positions and the weak-side players occupy the two inside positions (see Figure 4-8). As shown in Figure

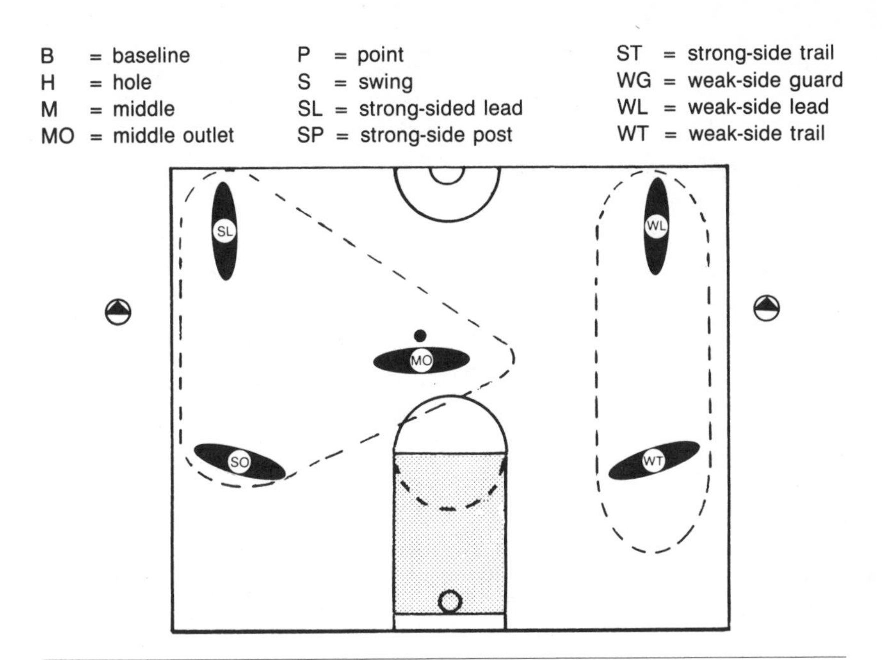

Figure 4-6 The Strong-Side and Weak-Side Positions in the Outlet Set.

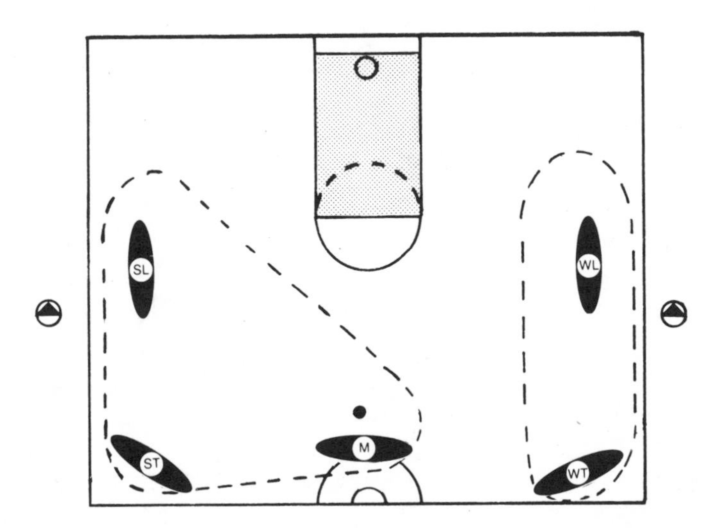

Figure 4-7 The Strong-Side and Weak-Side Positions in the Midcourt Set.

4-9, the fast break triangle phase of the basic full court set consists of three positions in the triangle and two trail positions. The three triangle positions are the point (P), the base-

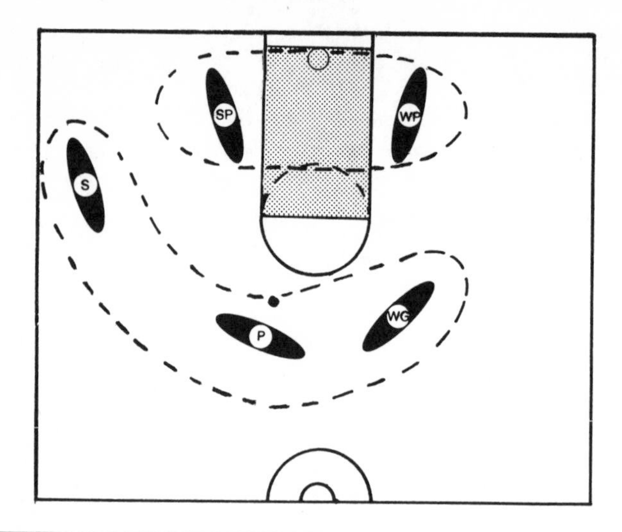

Figure 4-8 The Perimeter and Inside Positions in the Frontcourt Set.

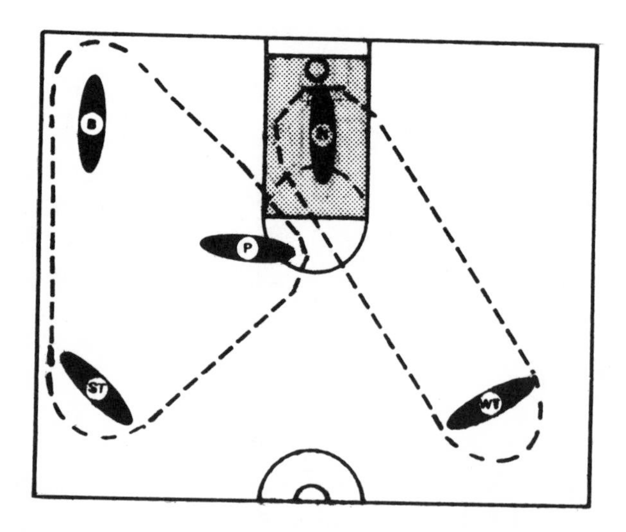

Figure 4-9 The Strong-Side and Weak-Side Positions in the Fast Break Triangle.

line (B), and the hole (H). The two trail positions are the weak-side trail (WT) and the strong-side trail (ST). Strong-side players occupy the point, the baseline, and the strong-side trail positions. Weak-side players occupy the hole and weak-side trail positions.

In the backcourt, when players move to occupy positions in an outlet set, they should stay near the center of the middle lane until they have cleared the top or the head of the key. Staying near the center of the court makes it easier for players to switch assignments. When players stay near the center of the court, they can more easily see which teammates are ahead of them than when they are scattered in all three lanes. As a result, trailing players can more easily see whom they are trailing. This is an important point because trailing players should key on the leading players who have priority in selecting positions. As a result, when a lead player moves to occupy a position, any player or players assigned to the same group of positions on a first-come, first-served basis must read this action and move to occupy other positions in the group.

Knowing the Tasks Assigned to Each Position

When your players occupy positions in an offensive set, they should know the role of the positions they occupy. You should define the role of each position in terms of tasks. As described on pages 5 and 7 in chapter 1, these tasks include making decisions, executing play options, and maintaining system integrity. Because a player occupying a position will either have the ball or not have the ball, the tasks of each position relate to playing with or without the ball. As a result, when a player occupies a position, for example, in a frontcourt set, he or she must know the decisions, the play options, and the various aspects of maintaining system integrity that are involved in playing with and without the ball in that position.

Knowing the Cues and Where to Look for Them

Before each game, your players should know the array of event-related, team-related, and opponent-related cues that will help them play effectively against their opponents. For example, your players should know the style and the characteristics of the types of defenses the opposing team is likely to use. This information, along with information about the characteristics and preferences of opposing players on defense, provides valuable cues. Cues may be changed or added as play unfolds. For example, you may want to make some change if a team uses a new defense or you learn that a particular opponent is hurt.

During each moment of play, each player on offense should have an overview of what is happening on the court. The player should know what the player guarding him or her is doing as well as the location, movement, and actions of his or her teammates and their opponents. For example, a player who is advancing the ball with a dribble should know what the opponent guarding him or her is doing as well as what his or her teammates and their opponents are doing. This overall picture of what is happening helps players select play options and maintain system integrity. If asked, a player should be able to paint an accurate word picture of what is happening on the court at any moment during play. Many players find this difficult; I have had some who were hard pressed even to tell me the color of the opposing team's uniforms.

Within that overall picture, players must be able to focus on particular aspects of play. You must, as a result, organize the offensive structure so that players will know which teammate or teammates to key on for cues as play unfolds. For example, each time a player gets the ball in my outlet set, he or she will look first to execute a penetrating pass. As a result, should a player get a defensive rebound, he or she will look first to pass to the middle outlet. The player with the ball will key on teammates and on their opponents.

Knowing the Principles of Play

Knowledge related to the principles of play includes (a) knowing the symmetry of each set, (b) knowing how to play with flow, (c) knowing the sequencing of movement and of play options, and (d) knowing the traffic rules.

Knowing the Symmetry of Each Set

To help your players focus their attention more on their opponents than on their own teammates, you must define the symmetry of each set. For example, as shown in Figure 4-10, when a weak-side player gets a defensive rebound, he or she occupies the rebound position where he or she rebounds. The middle outlet (MO) position is located in the center of the middle lane as deep as circumstances dictate. Generally, it is located somewhere between the head of the key and the restraining circle at center court. Both the strong-side and the weak-side leads (SL and WL) are located 15 to 25 feet ahead of the middle outlet. The side outlet (SO) is located in the same sidelane as the strong-side lead along a line extending from the head of the key. All the positions in the side lanes are about six feet from the sidelines. In all entries related to the outlet set, the location of the three strong-side positions (the SL, MO, and the SO) is always in the same half of the court as the ball.

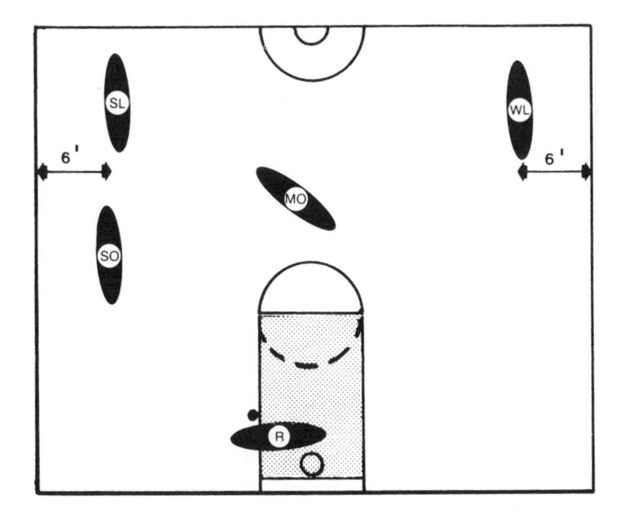

Figure 4-10 Keeping Symmetry in the Outlet Set When the Weak-Side Player Gets a Rebound.

Knowing this symmetry, each player should know where he or she and his or her teammates should be in relation to the court grid, to each other, and to the opposing players. Although each of your players should be able to draw the general formation of positions of each offensive set, the actual location of each position in a set during play results from your players reading a variety of cues. Therefore, although the actual formation will have the same general shape as the conceptual formation, the players will continuously modify it to meet the immediate needs of play. During the course of a game, your players will play closer together or farther apart to reduce or increase the length of the passing lanes.

How far apart your players are from each other is determined by balancing the need for spreading the defense and for facilitating quick player and ball movement from one position to another. Your players must spread the defense so that one opponent cannot guard two of your players. On the other hand, your players should not play so far apart that they create passing lanes that are too long. The longer the passing lane, the

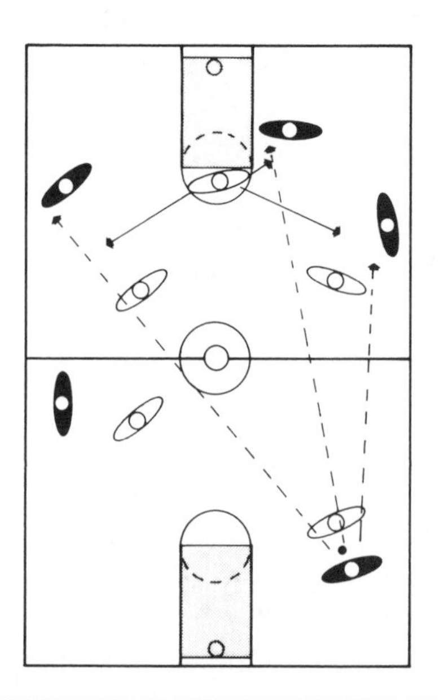

Figure 4-11 Too Many Long Passing Lanes.

more easily a defensive player can interfere with a pass or block more than one passing lane (see figure 4-11).

Maintaining symmetry also facilitates flow in play. How quickly the ball or a player moves from one position to another depends primarily on how far they must travel from one position to the next. If too far, the flow of play is disrupted each time one player has to wait for another player to occupy a position.

Knowing How to Play With Flow

If the offensive play of your team is to have a high degree of flow, you must give your players the knowledge that will help them to play in such a way that the ending of one movement or play option is the beginning of the next. For example, getting a defensive rebound is the first component of executing an outlet pass. Similarly, receiving a pass is an integral part of shooting. Frequently, my players and I have been impressed by an opponent's shooting during a pregame warm-up only to find that player is unable to score in a game against a defense. This inability to score is often caused by an inability to integrate receiving a pass with shooting. In warm-ups, that player is able to take his or her time, bounce the ball several times, and so on.

Another important aspect of effective offensive team play is executing set transition with flow. Flow in set transition occurs when the time interval between play ending in one set and beginning in another is as short as possible. To achieve flow in this aspect of team play, you must organize your players' movements and actions so that ending play in one set signals the beginning of play in another set. As described in chapter 2, in my full court set the ending of play in its fast break triangle phase cues the beginning of play in the frontcourt set. As shown in figure 4-12, players are in the fast break triangle phase as a player executes a dribble entry into the point position. His or her failure to shoot or pass immediately after ending the dribble cues transition from the full court set to the basic frontcourt set (see Figure 4-13).

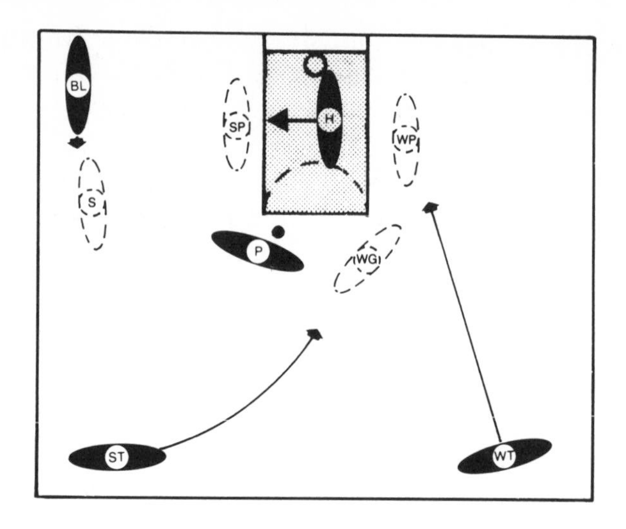

Figure 4-12 Transition From the Fast Break Triangle to the Frontcourt Set.

Knowing the Sequencing of Movement and of Play Options

If the offensive play of your team is to be organized so that, for example, all the players without the ball are not watching the player with the ball and calling for it at the same time, then the execution of each movement and play option assigned to each position must be ordered as play unfolds. This principle of play demands that you provide your players with the knowledge necessary to order their movement and their execution of play options. By knowing the sequencing of play options, a player with the ball will know which play option to initiate first. If this play option is a pass, the teammate who is occupying the position that you have sequenced to receive the pass should be open and ready for it at the moment the player with the ball is ready to pass. This knowledge also enables players to know what is likely to happen next and helps them to work in concert.

Knowing what is likely to happen next also helps players be ready to execute a particular movement or play option at the most opportune moment. As a result, if a player knows that he or she is responsible for executing a baseline throw-in after the opposing team scores a basket, that player can move to get the ball at the moment it enters the basket. Knowing what is likely to happen next will help your players keep playing after they complete the execution of a play option. Unlike football, basketball does not have huddles after each attempt to advance the ball. In offensive basketball play, therefore, your players need to know how to string movements and play options together until they lose possession of the ball. Therefore, when a player who arrives at the right place and time to receive a pass does not receive it, he or she must exit. This exiting cues the teammate who is sequenced next to cut (see Figure 4-13).

Figure 4-13 Sequenced Cutting. Player 3 Initiates a Cut, Using Player 5 as a Screen, and Player 1 Exits.

Knowing the Traffic Rules

A number of offensive principles of play serve as traffic rules for players. Some of them guide their movement. Others help them to select play options. For example, when an offensive player who is advancing the ball with a dribble approaches a teammate who is occupying a position, one of two things should happen in my system of play. The player who is being approached will either screen for the dribbler or clear (see Figures 4-14 and 4-15).

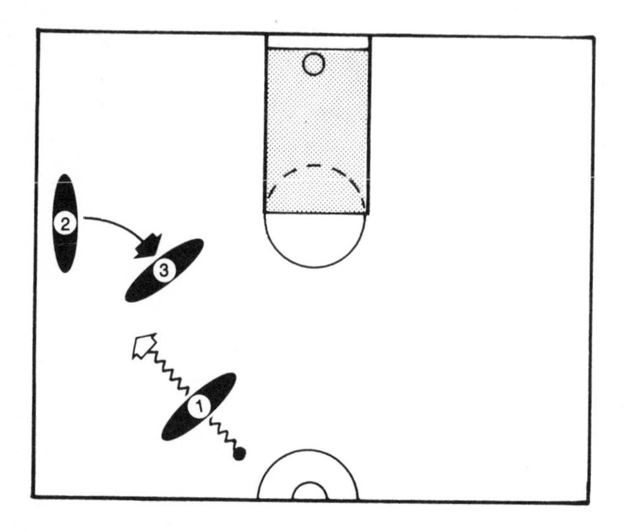

Figure 4-14 Screening for an Approaching Teammate.

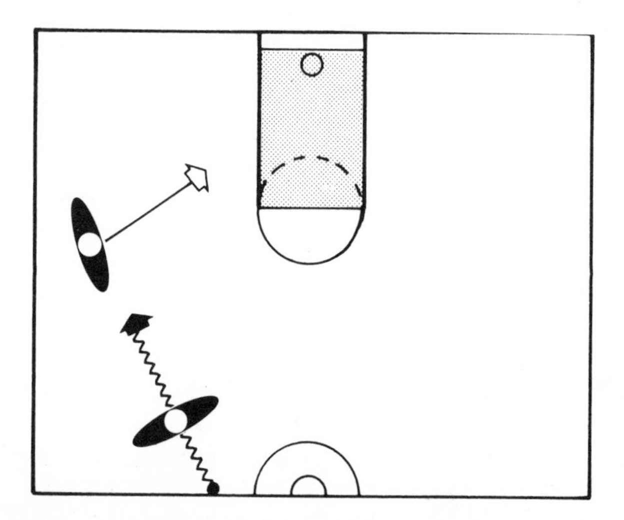

Figure 4-15 Clearing for an Approaching Teammate.

Players use another such principle of play to guide their actions in the basic frontcourt set. As shown in Figure 4-16, a perimeter player who is cued to basket cut may cut or set a screen for an adjacent perimeter player. Setting that screen cues the player for whom the screen is set to basket cut or use the screen (see Figure 4-17).

Figure 4-16 A Player Without the Ball May Either Call for It, Cut, or Screen.

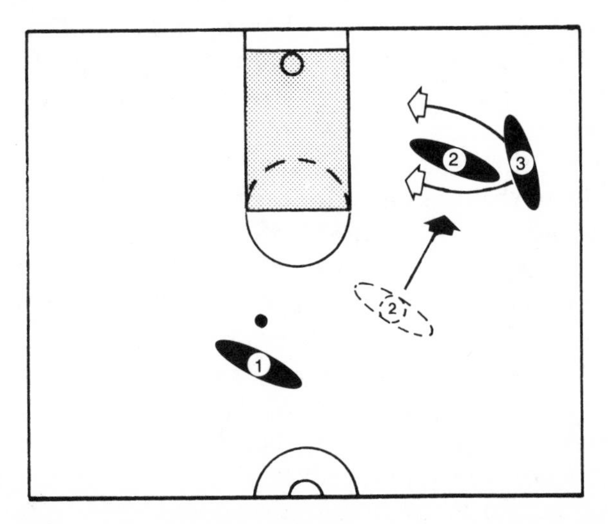

Figure 4-17 Choices: A Player for Whom the Screen is Set May Either Basket Cut or Use the Screen.

Undoubtedly, the two most important traffic rules in my system of play are penetrating and relaying. My players use these two principles to guide their movement and actions in every basic set. At the moment a player gains possession of the ball, he or she knows to penetrate, first with a pass and second with a dribble. Unable to penetrate, he or she will look to relay the ball to a teammate. As a result, each time a player gets possession of the ball, one or two teammates will be ready to receive a penetrating pass in the middle lane, and one or two teammates will be ready to receive a relay pass in the ball-side outside lane. For example, a player who gets a defensive rebound first looks to pass to a teammate who is executing a penetrating ball or basket cut. Then he or she looks to relay a pass to a teammate in the ball-side outside lane. If unable to execute either pass, the player with the ball will penetrate with a dribble.

Knowing How to Play Against the Defense

When players know the structure of their system of play and the principles of play that guide their movements and their actions within that structure, they are ready to play against the defense. If the system is coherent and complete, a player will be able to deal with any situation that is likely to occur at any moment during play. Such a system of play, however, provides players with general guidelines for their movements and actions, rather than with specific directions. Players are free to choose which particular movement or action to execute from a number of suitable movements and actions provided by the system. For example, in my system of play, an offensive player who is sequenced to execute a penetrating cut has the following range of options: (a) to ball cut, (b) to basket cut, or (c) to stunt with a teammate. He or she chooses the most suitable option to execute on the basis of reading event-related, team-related, and opponent-related cues. As a result, in a conceptual system of play, every offensive movement and action is predicated on choice. Having the ability to make choices, players have the potential to play with spontaneity, creativity and imagination.

Chapter 5

A Conceptual Approach to Defensive Team Play

Knowing the Importance of Defense

Youngsters who aspire to playing competitive team basketball often believe that basketball is a game of offense. They are misled by what they see at games, by what they see and hear when they watch a televised game, and by what the news media tell them. At games, nearly all the spectators watch the player with the ball; even players do this. When a game is televised, the camera and the announcers follow the ball. People from the media also generally focus their reporting on the high scorers.

When they practice on their own, players invariably work with a ball. In pick-up games, everyone wants the ball. Because of all the offensive readiness, one-on-one, and team skills that need to be learned and honed, teams spend at least twice as much time during practice working on offense than on defense.

Some teams do not play defense seriously but rely instead on their ability to outscore their opponents. Teams using this approach can be successful, providing their opponents also do not take defense seriously or, if they do, are inept on defense. Therefore, it is not surprising that many aspiring players work very hard on their offensive game, particularly on scoring, at the expense of their defensive game.

Youngsters should learn, however, that playing sound defense is as important as playing sound offense, for both individual and team success. Many players who were great scorers at one level of play have disappeared from the scene or have ended up "riding the pine" at a higher level because they could not or would not play defense. Most teams need only one or two great scorers. Indeed, teams can even get by without a great scorer. If teams want to win consistently, however, they need every player on the court to play sound defense.

Sound defense will help your team win in several ways. First, a sound defense will deny opponents high-percentage shots. A high shooting percentage on offense is directly related to getting open shots, shots that are close to the basket, and shots that players prefer taking.

Second, sound defense increases the probability of more opportunities for live ball phase transitions from defense to offense. These live ball transitions, like defensive rebounds, steals, loose balls, and intercepted passes, are excellent spring boards for high-percentage scoring opportunities. Throw-ins that result from turnovers and that are often the result of good defense also provide additional scoring opportunities.

Over the years, I have found that, as a rule, whether we won or lost, both teams made close to the same number of field goals. Any significant spread in scoring, therefore, resulted from those easy baskets that an ineffective defense allows.

Third, consistency throughout a game and a season can be achieved much more easily on defense than on offense. Teams that rely on players to score—particularly from the perimeter—are, in a sense, playing Russian roulette. Although a player may shoot a relatively high percentage from the perimeter over a season, a good shooter will be cold at times in a game and occasionally for an entire game. On the other hand, because sound performance is more likely to be consistent on defense than on offense, good defensive play can carry a team through those bad times when its offense is not up to par.

Qualities Needed to Play Effective Defense

Your players should play defense with their hearts and their heads. On defense, players need to be highly aroused. They must be tenacious, aggressive, and persistent in their efforts to interfere with the play of their opponents. However, their arousal must be disciplined. Their emotional batteries should be fully charged from the moment that they lose possession of the ball to the moment they regain it. However, players must use their powers of perception and intellect to direct this energy.

The rheostat that releases, directs, and stops the flow of this emotional energy is the knowledge of when, where, and how to attack the offense. For me, the relationship between defense and offense is like the relationship between the mongoose and the cobra. The mongoose knows how to kill snakes but does not do it in a hysterical or frenzied manner that would drain great quantities of energy unnecessarily. The mongoose executes its skill with dispatch at the precise moment that the snake is most vulnerable to attack. Like the mongoose, players on defense should always be ready and waiting to strike anywhere on the court grid, whenever chance or their opponents provide an opportunity.

Appearance and Reality

I have come to think that teams play only two kinds of defense: effective defense and ineffective defense. As a result, whether a team uses a man-to-man, a zone, a match-up, or a combination defensive set is of little consequence. No matter which defensive set a team uses, players must perform certain tasks that are an integral part of *effective defense* rather than of a particular defensive set. For example, someone will have to be responsible for the opponent with the ball. Someone else will have to be responsible for protecting the basket. The player who is protecting the basket and the remaining three players must be responsible for the opponents without the ball.

As a result, the differences between one defensive set and another are more a matter of form than of substance. For example, whether a team plays man-to-man or zone defense in the backcourt, it must be able to defend against penetrating drives and cuts.

Providing Defensive Balance

You must design your defensive structure so that while your players are on offense in any area of the court grid, they will be ready to play defense at the moment they lose possession of the ball. At that instant, one of them must protect the basket from easy lay-ups, another must be responsible for the opponent with the ball, and the remaining players must get in front of the ball, while picking up opponents to guard.

In my conceptual system, players provide defensive balance while on offense in specific ways. For example, the player occupying the baseline throw-in position in our outlet set is responsible for protecting the basket during the baseline entry pass. As a result, should a turnover occur during this entry, that player must protect the basket. If this entry succeeds, the player executing the pass will occupy the weak-side trail position, first in the outlet set and later in the midcourt set. Again, while occupying the trail position in both sets, one of his or her major tasks is to protect the basket at the moment a turnover occurs (see Figures 5-1, 5-2, and 5-3). The player closest to the ball at the moment the turnover occurs is responsible for the opponent with the ball.

Once the ball enters the frontcourt, two of the three perimeter players occupy the long and short safety positions at the moment a turnover occurs. The player occupying the

Figure 5-1 Protecting the Basket in the Backcourt.

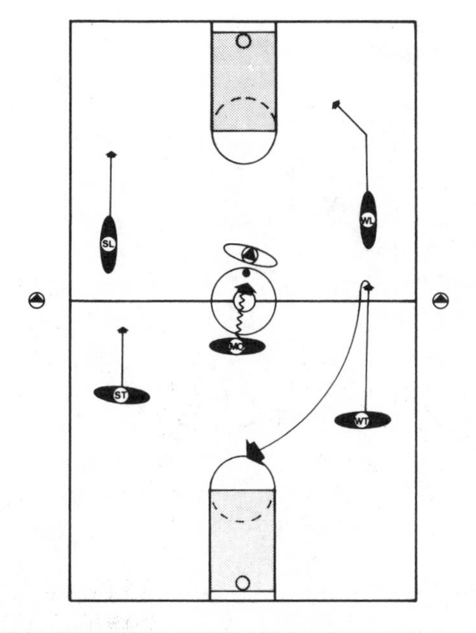

Figure 5-2 Protecting the Basket in Midcourt.

short safety position is responsible for the ball, and the player in the long safety position is responsible for protecting the basket (see Figure 5-4).

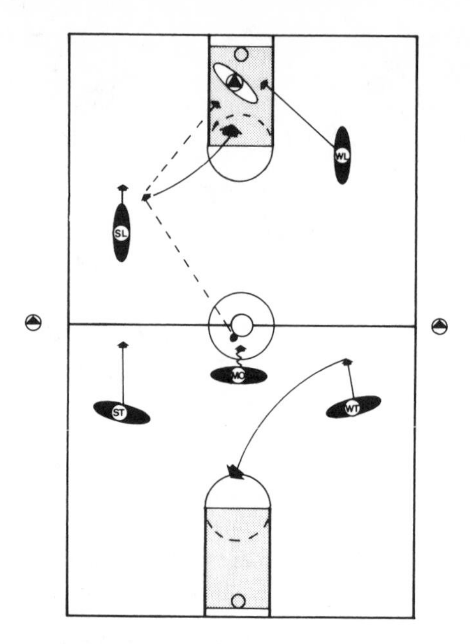

Figure 5-3 Protecting the Basket in Full Court.

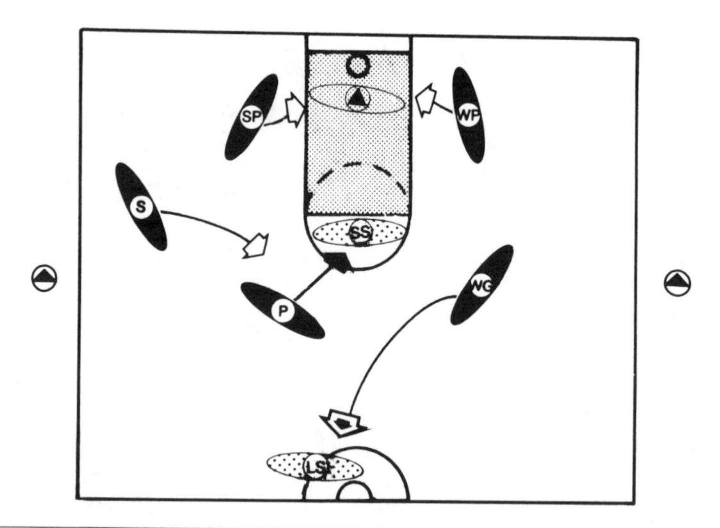

Figure 5-4 Providing Long (LS) and Short Safety (SS).

The prime responsibility for players in transition from offense to defense is stopping the fast break. Having stopped the opposing team from initiating a fast break, the defensive players must select (a) a defensive front, (b) a defensive set behind that front, and (c) positions in the selected set. Once organized in this way, they are ready to confront the offense. Phase transition entries initiated by a sideline or baseline throw-in tend to provide more time for the players on defense to get organized than do live ball entries such as a defensive rebound. For this reason, teams on defense are more likely to select a full court or three-quarter court front only after they score a field goal or a free throw.

Knowing Your Opponent

Having provided defensive balance so that each player on defense knows who is repsonsible first for the ball, second for protecting the bakset, and third for each player on offense, your team is ready to confront the offense—regardless of the front or the set behind the front. Of course, should the opportunity present itself, individual players, as they are in the process of getting organized, should attack the offense by intercepting passes or stripping a player of the ball.

Before confronting an opponent, however, each defensive player should know everything possible about each individual opponent and about the way the opposing players play team basketball. On the basis of this knowledge, the defensive players choose the place, the time, and the method to confront and interact with their opponents.

Preferences and Weaknesses

Knowledge about the offensive play of your opponents falls into two general categories—preferences and weaknesses. Preferences are those actions that players and teams like doing because they do them well. An offensive player, for example, may prefer to drive to the right. Thus the player guarding him or her should overplay the right hand, forcing the offensive player to dribble to the left. If a team has players who prefer to play inside, its offensive frontcourt set will likely be designed to get the ball inside. As a result, the defensive team should direct its strategy toward taking away the offense's inside game. A basic defensive principle of play, therefore, is taking away preferences or influencing the opposing team to play in certain ways.

Offensive weaknesses are those areas in which individual opponents and the opposing offensive system are deficient. Defensive players should look for every opportunity to exploit such weaknesses. Individuals may have physical, skill, and emotional deficiencies. For example, the player advancing the ball may be shorter than the players who are responsible for guarding him or her. As a result, when double-teamed, that player will have difficulty in throwing a high penetrating pass to the basket. This knowledge makes it easier for the other defensive players to cheat, particularly the player who is responsible for protecting the basket.

Two common offensive skill deficiencies that defensive players can exploit are (a) not seeing the defense when executing a pass and (b) being an arm passer. An arm passer is a player who commits to passing at the moment his or her arms begin their passing action. As a result, the execution of the pass occurs when the arms begin to move. Knowing this, a defensive player can wait for the pass by not blocking the passing lane and then moving to intercept the pass as soon as the passer begins arm action. If a player has both deficiencies, he or she is unlikely to complete many passes—unless, of course, the player guarding the intended receiver is not paying attention.

Being easily upset is another offensive deficiency. For example, I have seen good shooters lose their confidence if they miss their first shot, particularly if it was a shot they would normally make. Then they either stopped shooting or, having lost their confidence, shot poorly the entire game. As a player, I once had to guard an opponent who was a good perimeter shooter. Before the game, I told him that I was so concerned about checking him that I was not even going to try and stop his perimeter shooting. The first time he received a pass in a position from which he could usually score blindfolded, I stood back and left him unguarded. He shot and missed. He did not take another shot from the outside that night.

Your players should be constantly trying to exploit deficiencies in the offensive team play of their opponents. One such common deficiency is not involving all the players in the offense. A defensive player who perceives that he or she is guarding a player who is not involved in the offense can help his or her teammates who are guarding opponents who are involved. For example, after making an entry pass in their frontcourt set, many point guards will stay outside effective shooting range. When the ball returns, these players are not a serious scoring threat, and the players guarding them can cheat and help their teammates on defense (see Figure 5-5).

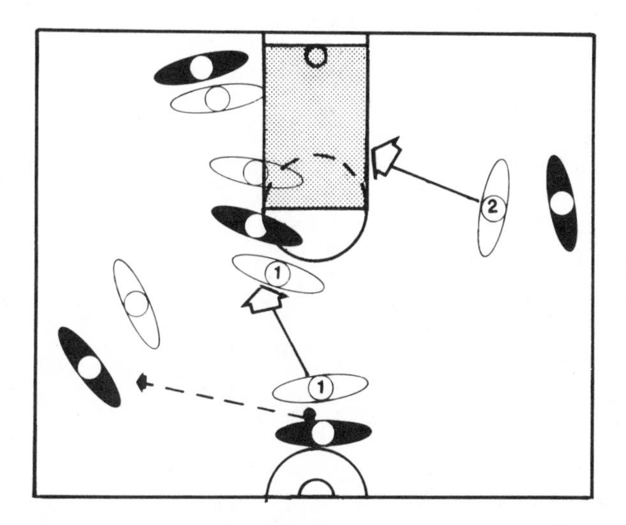

Figure 5-5 Exploiting a Player Who is Not Involved in the Offense.

Selecting a Defensive Front and a Defensive Set

After providing defensive balance, your players must be able to select a suitable defensive front and a defensive set to play behind that front. A number of event-related cues can help them make their selection. For example, scoring a field goal or a free throw may cue the selection of a 1:2:1:1 defensive zone set behind a three-quarter front (see Figure 5-6). The ball crossing the center line may cue transition from that set to

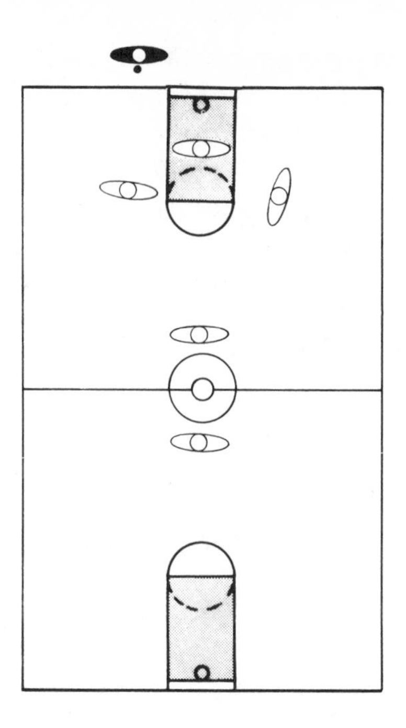

Figure 5-6 Selecting a 1:2:1:1 Zone Set Behind a Three-Quarter Front.

a backcourt man-to-man set. All other phase transition entries by the offensive team in their backcourt, like a defensive rebound, may cue players to select a man-to-man set behind either a midcourt or a half-court front.

Of course, during the course of the game, your team should be able to vary their defensive fronts and sets, particularly if doing so may create difficulties for the opposing team. Some teams have different offensive sets for different defenses. Others may use the same set but change the movement and the actions of the players. Often these changes are directed by the coach. I can recall numerous occasions when the opposing coach would call for a time-out immediately after we changed our defense. After making the appropriate adjustments to their offense, they would return to the court ready to attack our defense only to discover that we were no longer doing what we were doing when they called the time-out.

Selecting Positions in a Defensive Set

After they have selected a set behind a defensive front, your players must know how to occupy positions within each set. Regardless of the front or the defensive set, one player must be on the ball and one player must protect the basket. As a result, when playing a zone set, players must immediately occupy the position closest to the ball and the position that affords the greatest protection to the basket. Suppose, for example, that a player assigned to one of the top positions of a 2:1:2 zone is the player closest to the basket at the moment phase transition is anticipated. In that case, he or she must occupy the middle position in the zone—which is always between the ball and the basket—until a teammate designated to play that position releases him or her.

When players select a man-to-man set, their first priority is to guard the player with the ball and the opponent closest to the basket. Unfortunately, defensive players may be required to guard an opponent with whom they are mismatched in terms of height, skill, or quickness, especially during a live ball phase transition in which the tempo of play is fast. When this situation occurs, the defensive player suffering the mismatch must quickly find a teammate with whom to switch opponents.

Assigning Players to Positions

My method for assigning players to positions in a defensive set is similar to that used in an offensive set. I assign players both to groups of positions and to particular positions. When I designate players to a particular group of positions, they are free to occupy positions within that group on a first-come, first-served basis. If a player is assigned to play only one position, only he or she may play that position, except when stunting occurs. For example, in a 2:1:2 zone set behind a backcourt front, two players may be assigned to play the two top positions on a first-come, first-served basis. On the other hand, four players may be assigned to play the two top and the two back positions on a first-come, first-served basis.

If the opposing team uses a 1:3:1 offensive set in the frontcourt, three players might be assigned to guard the three perimeter players on a first-come, first-served basis, one player assigned to guard the high post, and one player assigned to guard the other post.

Knowing How to Select a Position

Selecting a position in a zone set is different from selecting one in a man-to-man set. In a zone set, the positions are located in a particular formation. Although the location of each position in a zone will be influenced by the location of opponents in the area, the formation of each set is relatively fixed. As a result, when players look for a position in a zone set, they look for it in a particular location on the court grid.

In a man-to-man set, the location of each position is contiguous to the location of a particular opponent. As a result, the formation of a man-to-man set takes on the shape of the offensive formation. Therefore players occupy a position in a man-to-man set at the moment they select an opponent to guard.

Knowing the Tasks of Each Position

Having occupied a position in either a zone, man-to-man, match-up, or combination set behind either a full court front, three-quarter court front, a half-court front, a midcourt front, or a backcourt front, a player must know all the tasks assigned to all the positions in that set. Knowing the tasks of all the positions allows players to integrate and coordinate their efforts to interfere with the play of their opponents. These tasks include making decisions, executing play options, and maintaining system integrity. They fall into two general categories—guarding a player with the ball and guarding a player without the ball. For example, when a player is guarding a player with the ball in a man-to-man set, he or she should know all the appropriate movements and actions for interfering with the play, according to where the players and ball are in the court grid. He or she should also know the appropriate movements and actions for his or her teammates who are guarding opponents. The other team members should, in turn, know what the player guarding the player with the ball should be doing during each moment of play.

Knowing How to Read Cues

Having occupied a position in a defensive set, each player must look for relevant team-, opponent-, and event-related cues that will guide his or her movements and actions. Although defensive players should know as much as possible about what is happening on the entire court, they must key on those teammates, opponents, and events that provide the most relevant cues about what is likely to happen next. This foreknowledge enables your players to be prepared for what is likely to happen and to influence what is likely to happen as well.

The five players on defense are like a dragon with the player on the ball as the head and the other players as the body. Because the head directs the body, the players off the ball key on the interaction between the opponent with the ball and their teammate who is guarding him or her. The players off the ball must also key on the opponent or opponents for whom they are responsible.

The four players who make up the body adjust their location on the court in relation to the interaction between the "head" and the opponent with the ball, the opponent or opponents they are guarding, and the basket. All five players on defense strive to keep the ball from penetrating the body of the dragon.

In addition to reading cues that signal the selection of defensive fronts, defensive sets behind those fronts, and positions in each defensive set, players must learn to read cues that signal (a) changes in defensive pressure, (b) the selection of defensive play options, and (c) changes in position location and movement.

As with the movement and actions on offense, player movement on defense must be consistent with the defensive principles of play. Your players, therefore, must learn to use these principles to guide their movement and actions in each position they occupy in a defensive set. At any moment of play, a player should be able to explain his or her location on the court grid—for example, in terms of the symmetry of a particular defensive set.

Cues That Change Defensive Pressure

There are a number of cues for applying and removing pressure. Perhaps the most common cue is the entry. An attempt by the offensive team to execute an entry can be a cue for applying pressure. For example, many teams begin play in their frontcourt offense with a guard to forward entry. The cue for applying pressure could be the guard ending his or her dribble in preparation for the entry pass. Ending the dribble, therefore, cues the dragon to apply pressure in three ways. First, the "head" plays tight and aggressive defense on the player with the ball, thus denying the passing lane to the basket. Second, the defensive player guarding the forward on the ball side overplays and denies any pass. Third, the player guarding the post fronts, and the two offside defensive players should block passing lanes. Away from the ball, the player guarding the offside forward would be responsible for protecting the basket (see Figure 5-7).

A successful entry may also be a cue for removing defensive pressure. After scoring a basket, a team might challenge the baseline throw-in by having a defensive player on the ball and each of the other players front an opponent (see Figure 5-8). Thus, the dragon would work very hard to deny the baseline entry. Once that entry was made, however, the players would stop fronting.

At the moment the players become a dragon, they are ready to confront the offense. The intensity with which the dragon confronts the offense should vary. At times, this confrontation should be calm, even passive. At other times, it should be as aggressive, tenacious, and persistent as the rules and the referees will allow.

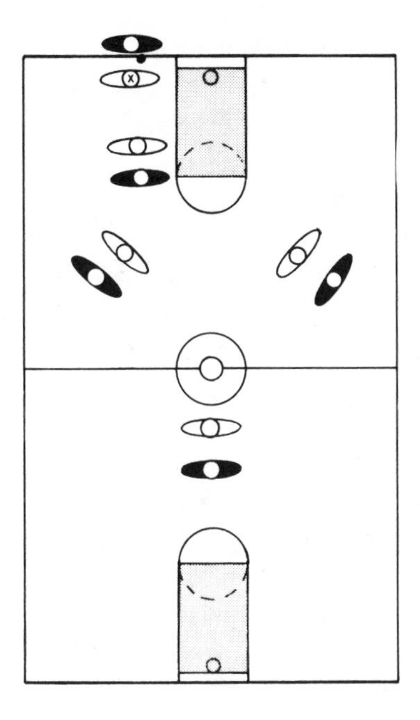

Figure 5-7 Applying Full Court Defensive Pressure.

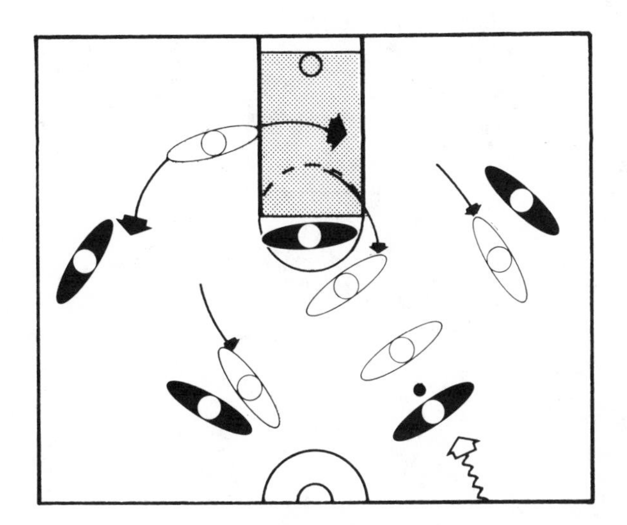

Figure 5-8 Applying Defensive Pressure in the Backcourt.

The dragon can play pressure or passive defense over the entire court grid or behind a particular front. As the opponents advance the ball toward their basket, the intensity of the defense can change several times. Whenever possible, increases in defensive intensity should be sudden and unpredictable. Putting pressure on opponents when they least expect it is the best way to create confusion and panic.

In a passive defense, a team does not challenge or confront the opposing team. Instead, the dragon works to influence the movement and the actions of the opponents in a manner that will take away individual and team preferences and exploit individual and team weaknesses.

While influencing, its head and body parts are waiting for opportunities to intercept a pass, to strip an opponent of the ball, and to execute a double team. The dragon also is patient. Patience and restraint are often rewarded with a turnover. For example, many times when an offensive team is confronted with a passive zone set behind a three-quarter or a full court front, the player with the ball who is not closely guarded will attempt a long pass down court to a teammate who is also

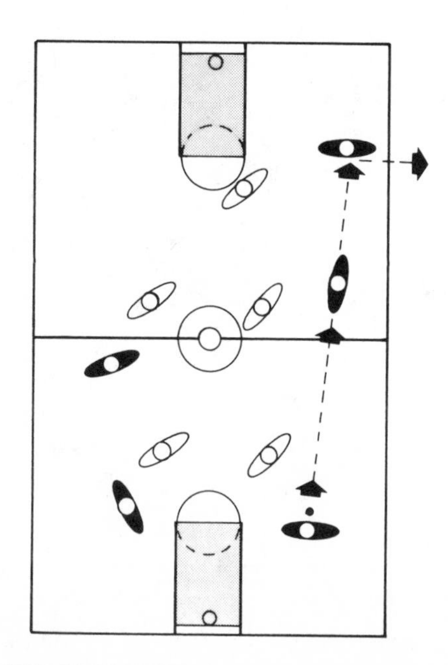

Figure 5-9 Using Passive Defense to Invite an Offensive Miscue.

not closely guarded (see Figure 5-9). Many of these passes result in a turnover. This occurs either because the passer throws the ball out-of-bounds or because the ball moves out-of-bounds off the receiver's hands.

Pressure defense is a high-risk defense because the basket is often left unprotected. During these moments, the player with the ball will have many opportunities to take the ball to the basket with a drive or to pass the ball to a teammate who is basket cutting. As a result, pressure defense is most effective when the "head" of the dragon can stop the player with the ball from executing either a penetrating pass or a drive toward the basket. Such a situation gives the players off the ball the best conditions for blocking passing lanes.

Because a player who ends a dribble cannot dribble again, a player who neither shoots nor passes immediately after ending a dribble—particularly when guarded by a taller player—is most vulnerable to pressure defense. Thus the best time to double-team an offensive player with the ball is after he or she

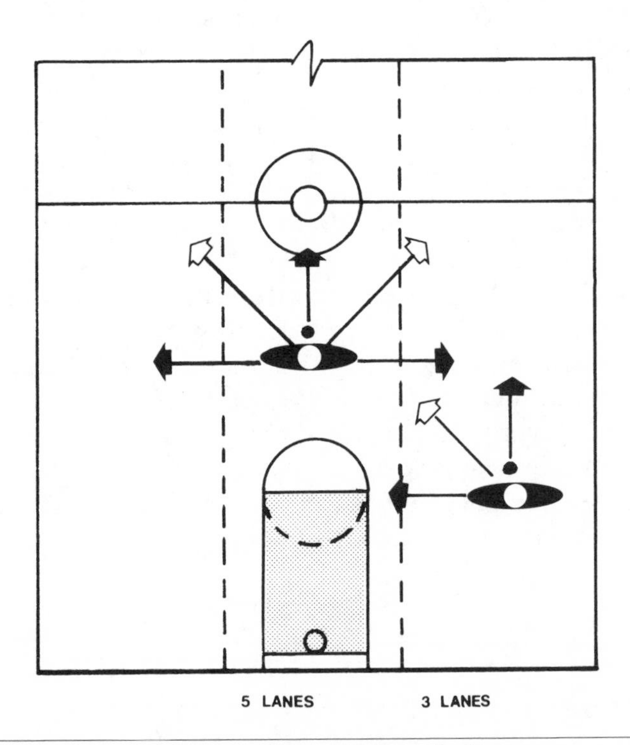

Figure 5-10 Using the Side Lanes to Double-Team.

begins to dribble. The best location on the court grid to double-team is near the sidelines. As shown in Figure 5-10, there are fewer passing lanes to guard when the ball is near a sideline than when it is in the center of the court.

Cues That Trigger the Execution of Play Options

Your players must know which cues trigger the selection of particular one-on-one or team play options. For example, you may know that an opponent prefers to pivot to his or her left to shoot after receiving a pass in the low post with his or her back to the basket. This is an opponent-related cue for the defense to influence him or her to pivot to the right.

Double-teaming is one of the most effective team play options a defense has. In full-court play or in the perimeter of the frontcourt, for example, a cue for double-teaming an opponent who is dribbling is "closing the door." Depending on how defensive play is organized, either the player guarding the dribbler or a teammate of the player guarding the dribbler can "close the door." When a player who is guarding a dribbler chooses to "close the door," he or she will place him or herself directly in the path of the dribbler suddenly and without warning. This action will bring a teammate who has been forewarned to administer the other half of the double team. The dragon now has two heads. At other times, the defensive player guarding the dribbler may lead the dribbler to a teammate who "closes the door." In both instances, the other defensive players become the triangular shaped body of the dragon (see Figures 5-11 and 5-12).

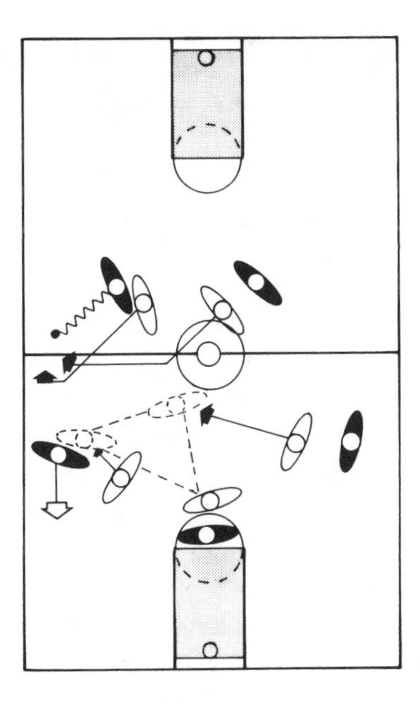

Figure 5-11 The Player on the Ball Cues a Double-Team.

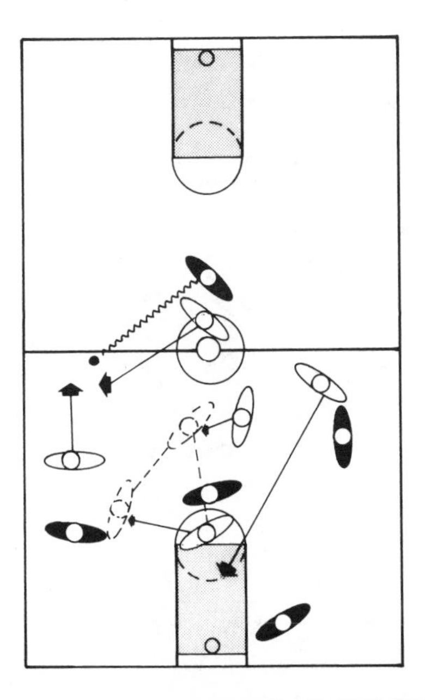

Figure 5-12 A Player off the Ball Cues a Double-Team.

Cues that Signal Changes in Position Location and Movement

My system of play has an ordinal process for reading cues that players use to monitor their location and their movement while they are occupying a position in a defensive set. First, the symmetry of each defensive set should guide their selection of playing positions and adjustments in the location of those positions on the court grid. For example, a player may choose to occupy the middle position in a 2:1:2 zone set behind a backcourt front. The symmetry of that set will dictate that the player is always directly between the ball and the basket at a point about two-thirds the distance from the basket to the ball when the ball is at the perimeter (see Figure 5-13). The player occupying this position, therefore, will continually adjust the location of the middle position by reading the distance of the ball from the basket so that he or she will always be about two-thirds of the distance from the basket to the ball. The player will also react to the movement of the ball as opposing players pass it around the perimeter so that he or she

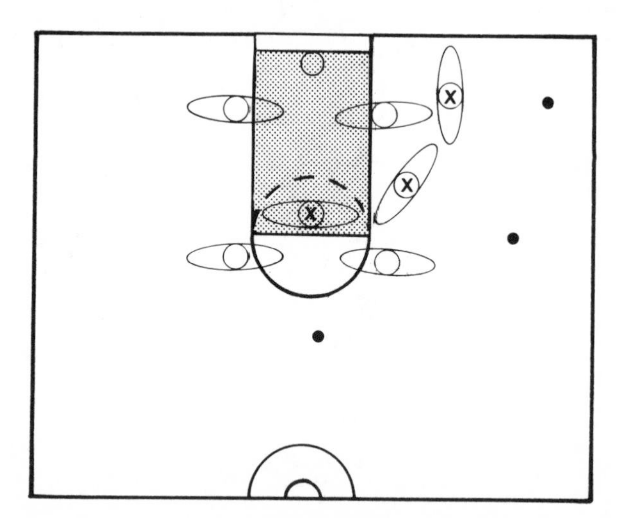

Figure 5-13 Playing Between the Ball and the Basket.

will be between the ball and the basket. Second, any changes in location or movement must be consistent with such other principles of play as initiating, influencing, dropping to the ball, and helping and recovering (see chapter 3). Third, within the context of position location and movement determined by set symmetry and the other principles of play, players must make further adjustments based on (a) reading what their opponents and teammates are doing and (b) knowing the limitations of their teammates, their opponents, and themselves.

Chapter 6

Helping Players to Play Conceptual Basketball

The Role of the Coach

Coaching is a tremendous responsibility because it is the single most important factor in determining how basketball is played. Coaches select players, teach a variety of skills, and determine systems and styles of play, game strategy, and player floor-time. They also must deal with the less tangible aspects, such as fostering dedication, courage, and the desire to play well. The main responsibility of coaching, however, is to help players to play basketball well.

In competitive basketball, playing well requires players to strive to win and to play with discipline. Striving to win releases all their powers of heart, spirit, and body, while playing with discipline calls on their powers of will and intellect. These twin qualities of release and restraint provide a complete test for these human capacities.

To help players play well, a coach must do a number of things. In my view, the most important of these tasks are (a) giving players a mission, (b) giving players the "plague," (c) helping players in practice, and (d) helping players in games.

Giving Players a Mission

To be successful, a team must perform many skills and play options well. It must also be lucky, which means avoiding injury or sickness at critical times over the season or getting the "breaks" during games. The cornerstone of success, however, is having clearly defined goals that all members agree on and commit themselves to achieving. This commitment to a mutually shared purpose sustains all members of the team through the difficulties, the challenges, and the heartbreak of a season of competitive basketball. This commitment also enables them to put the welfare of the team ahead of their own.

If the team's mutually shared purpose is to play well, you, the coach, must know and understand what your players need to play well. You must then organize this knowledge into a conceptual system of play that you can share with them. They must believe that you will help them become better players. Such an open and positive attitude is a necessary condition for optimum learning. They must also commit themselves to becoming the best players that they can possibly be.

You can begin developing a conceptual system of play by formulating an overview of the system. Years ago, I saw a television program in which an artist explained an approach to painting a landscape. She began with the general aspects. She drew a line across the canvas where the sky met the land and roughed in some peaks with a stream flowing from them. Only after she was satisfied with the location and the proportions of all the parts of the landscape did she turn her attention to the details.

Like the artist, you should first design the overall structure of your system of play, adding detail only within the context of that structure. This approach provides the best guarantee for developing a coherent structure.

You should begin by designing offensive and defensive sets that serve as the overall framework for team play. Then you can detail the rest of the system. Thus the design of each discrete part of the structure will be an integral part of the overall design. For example, the way you want a player to hold the ball should reflect how you want him or her to shoot. And how you want that player to shoot should be consistent with how he or she should play one-on-one basketball. Finally, the player's one-on-one play should be consistent with how you want him or her to play team basketball.

Your design of the overall structure as well as of each discrete part must adhere to the principles of play of your system. As a result, the way your players shoot should be dictated by clearly stated principles that serve as design specifications. In my system of play, for example, the technically sound movement pattern I have developed for shooting resulted from wanting players to shoot (a) quickly, (b) when closely guarded, (c) with suitable arc, and (d) softly. A suitable arc is one that presents the ball with the biggest target. Soft shots that hit the rim are more likely to go in than are hard shots. Unlike shots with flat arcs, shots with suitable arc that hit the rim tend to rebound vertically. Thus shots with suitable arcs provide better offensive rebounding opportunities near the basket than do hard shots, which are likely to bounce farther from the basket.

Giving Players "The Plague"

Before players can know how well they played, they must have a concept of good play against which to judge their performance. I have found that developing such a concept is difficult and frustrating for players; thus I have called the experience of becoming conscious of a conceptual system of play *catching the plague*. This plague of consciousness makes players aware of their deficiencies. For many of them, this awareness can be a difficult and frustrating experience.

Players who play conceptually know if they are playing well or badly. After executing a play option, such players get immediate feedback on how closely their performance matches their concept of how that option should be executed. On the one hand, players can become frustrated when their performance, though effective, continually falls short of their expectations. On the other hand, the experience of doing something the way it should be done and knowing that you have done it so affords the ultimate experience in exhilaration, joy, and satisfaction. One such experience is burned indelibly in my mind. A player who had just "caught the plague" was going through bad times because her shooting within the context of one-on-one play was not what we had agreed it should be. In games, her protruding lower lip and glowering eyes would signal her displeasure when she failed to execute correctly this particular play option. Finally, however, she succeeded in shooting correctly and immediately exclaimed "I did it!" in a voice bursting with satisfaction, joy, and exhilaration. I have never seen her happier. Of course, one of the satisfactions of coaching is being able to experience such moments, albeit vicariously.

The degree of consciousness players have of an overall system of play falls on a continuum that extends through three distinct levels. At the lowest level, the players' thoughts and actions are not governed by a system of play. Although the players may adhere to the rules of the game and display the beginnings of organized play, their play is more a function of aggressiveness, athletic ability, and individual initiative than of an overall plan. Although some players may exhibit readiness and one-on-one skills, very little evidence is shown of any sophisticated team play.

At the middle level of consciousness, players *are* aware of a system of play. At times, the system may be very sophisticated indeed. At this level, however, the system is personified in the coach. The players, therefore, know the system only through their coach. Their relationship is somewhat like that of the puppeteer and the puppets. The thoughts and actions of the players during the course of play are governed not by a system of play, but by their coach.

At the highest level of consciousness, the players know and understand a system of play that they have agreed to follow. In a game, therefore, the players are free to use their imagination and creativeness—spontaneously responding to situations with which chance or their opponents confront them, provided that their movement and actions are consistent with their system of play.

Helping Players in Practice

Coaches should use team practices for training, learning, and game preparation. Training involves honing and fine tuning readiness, one-on-one, and team skills that have been learned. Learning involves acquiring new skills and/or reshaping old ones. In preparing for an upcoming game, the players learn a game plan that provides information about their opponents and a strategy for attacking their defense and interfering with their play on offense.

At practices, the coach is a teacher. To fulfill this role, you must create a learning environment that will help players to perform to their fullest powers of heart, spirit, will, intellect, and body. In this environment, you should help players by (a) making them "free," (b) involving them in their own learning, and (c) painting the big picture for them.

Making Players "Free". The coach should instill in players the desire to be free—not free in the sense that they can do as they please but rather free from the limitations of preference. A player who is free to do as he or she pleases will want to do only those things that are comfortable or that bring immediate success. These players are prisoners of preference. For example, most righthanded players want to dribble with their right hand.

A player who wants to be free will strive to master all the skills of the game. Each time such a player masters a new skill, he or she becomes more free. A player is free, therefore, to the extent that he or she lacks limiting preferences. For example, a player who is able to dribble equally well with either hand is more free than the player who prefers to dribble with only one hand.

Because of individual differences, not all players will perform all the requisite skills of basketball equally well. Nevertheless, the coach has a responsibility to encourage all players to develop all the skills of the game. Quality of performance is relative. For example, a tall, slow player who finds it very difficult to dribble against a shorter, quicker player may have no difficulty dribbling against another tall, slow player.

Although players should work hard to develop their skills, they should play within their limitations in games. Therefore, the tall, slow player with a high dribble should not dribble when guarded by a shorter, quicker opponent.

Involving Players in Their Own Learning. The coach should involve players in the process of improving their own performance so that ultimately their development as players will be self-directed. When players can direct their own learning and hone their own performance, learning and training can take place without the coach. In that case, a player can learn and train between practices and during the off-season.

Initially, players rely on their coach to communicate to them a clear mental image of the particular behavior that is desired. For a period of time, they will need the coach to monitor their performance and to provide feedback. Once a player can perceive whether or not his or her performance of a particular task matches that mental image of the task, the player will be able to monitor his or her own performance. For example, coaches should make players aware that they should dribble in the full court only after trying to advance the ball with a pass. Although players may know this principle of play, they often will unconsciously violate it. At first, they will rely on you to provide appropriate feedback. You must help them to learn first to become aware of such violations and second to look to pass before choosing to dribble.

Painting the Big Picture. An important strategy in providing players with mental images is being careful not to overload them with information. You must resist the temptation to be long-winded or to impress the listener with the complexity and extent of your knowledge of the game. When painting a mental picture, a coach should say what is most relevant in as few words as possible. Break each skill down into its component parts and determine the best order in which to present these parts for learning. When teaching new players what to do immediately after receiving a pass in the full court, for example, do not expect them to master all the related tasks simultaneously. Begin by identifying the most salient feature and insisting that their performance reflect this feature. Add more detail as players master the more salient aspects of the skill. For example, after receiving an outlet pass, a player should immediately look to the basket for a teammate.

Helping Players in Games. At games, the coach stops being a teacher. Games are for performing, not for learning.

As a result, your role at games is to support players by cajoling, encouraging, exhorting, and, when necessary, admonishing them. While supporting them, you are responsible for (a) making decisions and (b) monitoring individual and team performance.

Making Decisions. The coach is the decision-maker in games—the one responsible for directing overall team strategy. Although a player may suggest a particular course of action—for example, that the team employ a zone defense—the coach is responsible for making the decision. Should the coach decide to play zone, the decision is his or hers alone, regardless of the outcome.

Monitoring Individual and Team Performance. During the course of play, the coach must make sure that individual players and the team as a whole follow the game plan. When necessary, the coach will help players adjust their play to counter unforeseen strategies in the offensive and defensive play of the opposing team. I believe that coaches should never, however, attempt to introduce something new. It will rarely, if ever, work and is likely to adversely affect the performance of some players.

After each game, you must evaluate individual and team performance. On the basis of that evaluation, you should modify training and learning programs for individual players and the team.

When evaluating performance, coaches are often tempted to attribute losses or poor performances to bad luck, injuries, bad officiating, inadequacies of players, and coaches who send him or her unskilled players. Such behavior is nonproductive. After all, a coach has no control over luck and little or no control over other people's actions. What you can best control is your coaching. Therefore you should spend your time evaluating yourself to ensure that you are doing everything you can to help players perform to their full potential.

Measuring Success

Coaches should know how to measure the quality of their coaching. Winning is an unreliable measure. Too many variables affect winning, such as injuries, the availability of gifted athletes, and chance.

Similarly, winning is an unreliable measure of the quality of team play. The final score decides who wins the game but not necessarily which team plays better basketball.

Because a coach has far better control over how his or her team plays basketball than over the outcome of a game, the quality of coaching should be measured by how well individual players and the team play basketball, as well as by how much they improve over time.

Unfortunately, however, success tends to be measured by winning—an understandable tendency as people can measure winning more easily than they can judge the quality of play. When I was a coach, friends or interested fans rarely asked whether we played well, only whether we had won.

Coaches who measure their success primarily by their win-loss record have difficulty teaching players how to play basketball and helping them play better. Learning is a difficult and slow process. When players are learning, their performance often deteriorates. As a result, in trying to win, many coaches rely on recruiting players with special skills or physical attributes, such as athletic ability and size, and on systems of play designed to hide individual and team weaknesses and highlight behavior players have already mastered.

Teams that depend on such an approach share a number of characteristics. They play zone rather than man-to-man defense. There is little, if any, fast break play on offense. The greater part of the dribbling and the playmaking is relegated to one or two players. The offense is oriented to set plays so that only select players shoot. This approach has the unfortunate effect of perpetuating player weaknesses and blocking further development of the more versatile and complete basketball player, which, in turn, precludes the highest form of team play.

If you are determined to develop complete players, you must be prepared to tolerate many mistakes as players learn. The only way players will learn to play effective man-to-man defense is to work on related skills in practice and use man-to-man in games. The only way players will learn fast break play is if you encourage them, when they have the ball in practice and in games, to be constantly alert for opportunities for advancing the ball quickly with a pass or a dribble. Coaching young players who are learning the game or experienced players who are refining play options is not easy. But you will find your job much easier and the rewards more satisfying as you apply concepts of basketball rather than regimented systems.

About the Author

Vic Pruden's basketball coaching career spans more than twenty-five years and includes experience at high school, club, provincial, university, and national levels, and with both men's and women's teams. His coaching record has been a highly successful one with only two seasons with a win/loss record of less than .500.

Vic was Director of Athletics at the University of Winnipeg for thirteen years. During that time he inaugurated both the men's and women's intercollegiate basketball programs. Both teams held excellent records, and during his years as the women's coach, the team won six out of seven conference championships and were national finalists twice. Another highlight of Vic's coaching career included two years working with junior age elite athletes, identifying and developing potential players for the national junior women's team.

Vic and his family live in Winnipeg where he also teaches high school. His leisure time pursuits include basketball coaching and clinics, politics, travel, and work with sports organizations.